THE DISC

THE DISCUSSION

A Reference Guide to the Theory Requirements
of LAMDA Graded Examinations in
The Speaking of Verse and Prose

Third Edition

Edited by Catherine Weate

PUBLISHED BY
OBERON BOOKS
FOR THE LONDON ACADEMY OF
MUSIC AND DRAMATIC ART

First published in 1996 in association with LAMDA Ltd.
by Oberon Books Ltd.
521 Caledonian Road, London N7 9RH
Tel: 020 7607 3637/Fax: 020 7607 3629
info@oberonbooks@btinternet.com
www.oberonbooks.com

Third edition 2004. Reprinted 2006.

ISBN: 1 84002 431 3

Cover design: Joe Ewart for Society

Printed in Great Britain by Antony Rowe Ltd, Chippenham.

Contents

GRADE 8 – GOLD MEDAL

John Burnside	55
T S Eliot	56
Lawrence Ferlinghetti	62
Philip Larkin	64
Edna St Vincent Millay	68
Pablo Neruda	72
Muriel Stuart	75
Jonathan Swift	77
Isabel Allende	80
Peter Carey	82
George Eliot	84
Henry James	87
Bernard MacLaverty	90
Rohinton Mistry	91
Dorothy Parker	94
Bram Stoker	96
William Shakespeare	100

Introduction

The Discussion is an essential reference guide for teachers and students of speech and drama which also provides information on the set theory for LAMDA *Graded Examinations in Speech: The Speaking of Verse and Prose 2004 – 2009.*

Graded Examinations in Speech: The Speaking of Verse and Prose

The examinations have been designed to develop the skills necessary for effective oral communication of the written word, including interpretative skills, technical skills and knowledge of literature. *The Discussion* should be read in conjunction with the specification for *Graded Examinations in Speech: The Speaking of Verse and Prose 2004 –2009,* which is available from LAMDA on request.

The examinations are divided into four distinct levels, in line with the National Qualifications Framework.

ENTRY LEVEL
ENTRY   MINIMUM AGE: 8 YEARS

LEVEL 1: FOUNDATION
GRADE 1   MINIMUM AGE: 9 YEARS
GRADE 2   MINIMUM AGE: 10 YEARS
GRADE 3   MINIMUM AGE: 11 YEARS

LEVEL 2: INTERMEDIATE
GRADE 4   MINIMUM AGE: 12 YEARS
GRADE 5   MINIMUM AGE: 13 YEARS

LEVEL 3: ADVANCED
GRADE 6 – BRONZE MEDAL   MINIMUM AGE: 14 YEARS
GRADE 7 – SILVER MEDAL   MINIMUM AGE: 15 YEARS
GRADE 8 – GOLD MEDAL   MINIMUM AGE: 16 YEARS

The set theory is listed in the 'knowledge' section of each grade within the specification.

The Discussion Format

The candidate's knowledge is tested in discussion with the examiner after the candidate has performed their pieces. The examiner will initiate the discussion and the candidate will be expected to respond. The discussion should evolve into a two-way exchange between the examiner and the candidate, during which the candidate will be given opportunities to expand on his/her responses.

The nature of the discussion is informal and the examiner will do his/her very best to set the candidate at ease. Questioning may seem more formal in the higher grades as the set knowledge requirements increase in technical difficulty.

There is a time limit for the discussion so the examiner may not be able to cover every aspect of the set knowledge. However, the candidate should be *prepared* to discuss any aspect of the requirements for the grade level being assessed and any previous grade levels.

Set Knowledge

The examiner will base his/her questions on the set knowledge requirement printed in the specification for *Graded Examinations in Speech: The Speaking of Verse and Prose 2004–2009*. This information should be made available to the candidate by their teacher so that the candidate is not surprised by questions raised in the discussion.

The set knowledge has been designed to ease the candidate into the technical aspects of performing verse and prose, increasing in difficulty as the grades progress.

Questions will be based on the following:

Entry

- The reasons behind the choice of selections

- The meaning of individual words in both selections.

Grade 1

- The mood, content and contrast between selections

- The reasons behind the choice of selections

- The meaning of individual words in both selections.

Grade 2

- The story and main characters of the book from which the prose selection has been taken.

Grade 3

- The fundamental differences between verse and prose

- The story and main characters of the book from which the prose selection has been taken.

Grade 4

- The story and main characters of the book from which the prose selection has been taken

- Phrasing (sense-groups, breath-groups, parenthesis)

- Pausing (sense pause, emphatic pause, rhythmical or metrical pause, suspensory pause, caesural pause, emotional pause). Definitions must be illustrated with examples from the chosen pieces where possible.

Grade 5

- The story and main characters of the book from which the prose selection has been taken

- Emphasis and modulation (which includes stress, volume, pace, rate, pitch, inflection, tone colour). Definitions must be illustrated with examples from the chosen pieces.

Grade 6 – Bronze Medal

- The story and characters of the book from which the prose selection has been taken

- Breathing, voice production, resonance and projection.

Grade 7 – Silver Medal

- The story and characters of the book from which the prose selection has been taken

- Metre and rhythm (iambic, trochaic, anapaestic, dactylic and spondaic rhythms). Definitions must be illustrated with examples from the chosen pieces where possible

- Specific verse forms (blank verse, free verse and sonnet form)

- Figures of speech (alliteration, assonance, onomatopoeia, antithesis, pun, simile, metaphor). Definitions must be illustrated with examples from the chosen pieces where possible.

Grade 8 — Gold Medal

- The story and characters of the book from which the prose selection has been taken and/or play from which the Shakespeare selection has been taken

- The writers' biographical details and the social/historical context of their writing.

Practical Application

Practical use of the theoretical knowledge will lead to a greater understanding of verse and prose in performance. It is therefore important that the candidate relates set knowledge to their performance as much as possible in the discussion with the examiner. This is particularly relevant at Grade Four (phrasing and pausing), Grade Five (emphasis and modulation) and Grade Seven (versification), where the candidate will be asked to illustrate the information with examples from their selected performance pieces whenever possible.

The content of this book has been written for the candidate so that it can be introduced as part of a practical class. It is only then that the student of speech and drama will be able to see the relevance and be able to fine tune the delivery of their performance work by balancing technical precision with the creative process.

Catherine Weate
Head of Examinations

Contributors

Entry

Questions will be based on the following:

- *The reasons behind the choice of selections*

- *The meaning of individual words in both selections.*

(Page 20 *Specifications for Graded Examinations*)

Choosing Verse

Making the right choice is important, so what do you need to consider? Obviously you will want to perform a piece of verse that you like, on a subject that you can appreciate. Choosing material that you can relate to will make it easier for you to share it. You may also enjoy the rhythm, the rhyme and the sounds of the words, which you can use in performance. As you will be speaking more than one poem, look for a contrast in mood – this will allow you to show your versatility.

The Meaning of Words

To speak a poem you must understand it. This means that you must be sure of the meaning of all the words. Sometimes you can try to guess the meaning of a word that is new to you but you may be wrong! Do check any word about which you are even slightly uncertain. Some words have more than one meaning and you can only tell which one you want from its context.

Grade One

Questions will be based on the following:

- *The mood, content and contrast between selections*

- *The reasons behind the choice of selections*

- *The meaning of individual words in both selections.*

(Page 23 *Specifications for Graded Examinations*)

Mood, Content and Contrast

You will have selected two pieces of verse that differ in either theme or mood so that you are able to display some contrast in performance. The examiner will want to discuss the mood and content of both pieces and the differences between them. Remember, it is possible to have two very different approaches to the same subject.

To prepare you should look at the way the pieces are written. How are they shaped on the page? Do they have a strong rhythm? Do they both use rhyme? What is their mood? One may be humorous, the other more serious; one could be scary and the other bright and cheerful. You may also enjoy the sounds of the words in a poem.

If you think about all these things you will feel confident in your discussion with the examiner.

Grade Two

Questions will be based on the following:

- *The story and main characters of the book from which the prose selection has been taken.*

The candidate must be prepared to discuss with the examiner any aspect of theory specified for previous grades.

(**Page** 23 *Specifications for Graded Examinations*)

Story and Character

When you have read your book, try to answer these questions:

What happens in the story?
Where and when is the story set?
Do you have a favourite part of the story?
Who are the main characters?
What do you think these characters are like?
How do the characters relate to each other?
Who is your favourite character and why?
How does the extract you are performing fit into the story as a whole?

If you think carefully about your answers to these questions you will feel confident when speaking with the examiner.

When discussing your book in the examination, remember to answer the examiner's questions as fully as possible.

Grade Three

Questions will be based on the following:

- *The fundamental differences between verse and prose*

- *The story and main characters of the book from which the prose selection has been taken.*

The candidate must be prepared to discuss with the examiner any aspect of theory specified for previous grades.
(Page 24 *Specifications for Graded Examinations*)

The Fundamental Differences between Verse and Prose

There are three main factors which make verse different from prose.

1. Prose is the ordinary form of written and spoken language. In English, words flow from the left side of a page to the right side of a page and are arranged into sentences and paragraphs. Verse is immediately recognisable on the page as the words are shaped and arranged into patterns. Verse may be broken up into stanzas but this is not essential.

   Examples of different verse patterns:

   Cat! by Eleanor Farjeon
   Constantly Risking Absurdity by Lawrence Ferlinghetti

2. Both prose and verse possess rhythm but verse rhythm is more distinct. Rhythm is the beat or pulse you can hear when you say the words. Sometimes the rhythm is arranged in a regular pattern of stressed and unstressed

syllables, which is known as metre. Verse rhythm can be very strong and easy to feel or quite gentle and subtle.

Examples of verse with a strong metrical rhythm:

The Song of the Mischievous Dog by Dylan Thomas
Water Music by Alison Chisholm

An example of verse with a more gentle rhythm:

A Hot Day by A S J Tessimond

3. Verse uses language in a different way from prose. Prose writing usually follows a logical sequence and a grammatical order. Verse often ignores this. Insignificant but grammatically necessary words may be omitted and the accepted word order may change. In some modern verse there is little or no punctuation and even a lack of capital letters! Verse may also make more use of figures of speech, such as similes and metaphors, than prose.

An example of verse with a very flexible use of language:

Hist Whist by E E Cummings

All of the verse examples can be found in *The LAMDA Anthology of Verse and Prose Volume XVI*.

Choose a different anthology and find your own examples of these features.

Grade Four

Questions will be based on the following:

- *The story and main characters of the book from which the prose selection has been taken*

- *Phrasing (sense-groups, breath-groups, parenthesis)*

- *Pausing (sense pause, emphatic pause, rhythmical or metrical pause, suspensory pause, caesural pause, emotional pause). Definitions must be illustrated with examples from the chosen pieces where possible.*

The candidate must be prepared to discuss with the examiner any aspect of theory specified for previous grades.
(Page 27 Specifications for Graded Examinations)

PHRASING

A 'phrase', in speech, consists of a group of words linked together by sense. Phrases are sometimes called 'sense-groups'.

Sense-Groups

Each sense-group introduces a fresh idea. The sense-group may be one word or a number of words. To break a sense-group is to destroy the sense.

Breath-Groups

Breath-groups and sense-groups frequently, but not necessarily, coincide. The breath-group represents the number of sense-groups that can easily be said on one breath. The ability to adjust breathing to meet the demands of the breath-group depends on an understanding of phrasing and breath control. Breath pauses may be longer than sense pauses and should occur where a longer pause is indicated by the text.

Parenthesis

Parenthesis is when a word, phrase or sentence is inserted as an explanation or afterthought into a passage which is grammatically complete without it. It is usually marked by brackets, dashes, or commas.

Parenthesis can be made clear in performance with a pause before and after and a change in pitch and pace.

PAUSING

In speech, a pause is when sound stops. There are many different types of pause which help the speaker or reader to bring meaning and mood to life.

The Sense Pause

The sense pause is used in connected speech to mark the sense and the end or beginning of a sense-group. It is sometimes referred to as oral punctuation, but this can be misleading as it would seem to imply that it is used in the same places as written punctuation, which is not always the case.

The Emphatic Pause

A pause for emphasis may be made before a word or phrase, after the word or phrase, or, for extra strong emphasis, both before and after the word or phrase. The word or phrase is therefore isolated and achieves prominence. Carefully timed, an emphatic pause will build suspense and climax. To hold an emphatic pause for too long will break the sense and alienate an audience.

The Emotional Pause

An emotional pause is when the voice is suspended by the strong working of the emotions. It must be used with great subtlety or it will sound over-dramatic and insincere.

Different line structures in verse which affect pausing

End-stopping

An end-stopped line is where the sense and rhythm undergo a cessation of sound or pause at the end of the line, often indicated by a punctuation mark.

Enjambment

Enjambment is when the sense of a line of verse continues onto the next line (the opposite of end-stopping).

Different types of pauses used in verse

The Rhythmical or Metrical Pause

Rhythmical pauses are used at the ends of lines of verse and between stanzas to indicate the form and pattern of the verse. These pauses should be timed with the rhythm of the verse. A metrical pause is also used when a line of verse is shorter than the surrounding lines so that a pause is needed to balance the rhythm and timing.

The Caesural Pause

A caesura is a slight pause which occurs mid-line, usually indicated by a break in sense and sometimes indicated by a punctuation mark.

The Suspensory Pause

When an enjambed line occurs the speaker needs to preserve the meaning without losing the rhythm or form of the verse. A suspensory pause solves the problem. The last word of the first line is suspended by pitch and length, in other words, a pause on the word itself. Therefore the speaker must continue on to the next line without a breath pause.

*   *   *   *   *   *   *   *

Now try to find examples in your chosen selections.

Grade Five

The candidate will have a short discussion with the examiner. Questions will be based on the following:

- *The story and main characters of the book from which the prose selection has been taken*

- *Emphasis and modulation (which includes stress, volume, pace, rate, pitch, inflection, tone colour). Definitions must be illustrated with examples from the chosen pieces.*

The candidate must be prepared to discuss with the examiner any aspect of theory specified for previous grades.
(Page 27 *Specifications for Graded Examinations*)

EMPHASIS

Emphasis is when a speaker attaches extra prominence to a particular word or thought. It can be achieved through:

1. Modulation (varying use of stress, volume, pace, pitch, inflection, tone colour and pausing)

2. Lengthening individual sounds

3. Intensity

For example, dramatic emphasis can be achieved by increasing the intensity of the breath force, building volume and widening the pitch range.

If there is *under emphasis*, speech becomes dull, flat and monotonous. Sometimes, in certain types of humour, it can be used effectively, but this should be thought of as a technique rather than the normal means of communication.

If there is *over emphasis*, speech becomes irritating and tiring to listen to.

MODULATION

Modulation refers to the variations in voice and speech used by the speaker to convey meaning and mood. This includes varying the use of stress, volume, pace, pitch, inflection, tone colour and pausing.

Stress

Stress is when prominence is given to a particular word or syllable, usually through a combination of extra breath force, a change in pitch and a lengthening of sound.

1. Word Stress

- Every word of more than one syllable has its own stress, for example: dragon

- Some words change meaning according to word stress, for example: subject/subject

- Compound words usually bear double stress, for example: homemade

2. Sentence Stress

When words are linked together, word stress changes under the influence of sentence stress. Sentence stress depends on two things:

- The relative importance of words in the sentence, depending on the context. The more important the word, the stronger its stress. For example:

  He told me his story quickly and with great enjoyment.

- The rhythm of the sentence. For example:

  homemade

  homemade jam

  it's all homemade

Volume

Volume refers to the level of loudness or softness with which words are spoken. There should be constant fluctuations of volume to create a well-modulated delivery but for most work (especially verse speaking) there should be only the gentlest crescendo and diminuendo. If too much breath force is used then shouting will occur. Shouting lacks subtlety and, if used for extended periods of time, creates vocal problems.

Pace

Pace variation is integral to the communication of meaning and mood. There should be constant fluctuations of pace to create a well-modulated delivery.

A slower pace can be achieved by lengthening vowels and continuant consonants and lengthening the space between words. Words suggesting size, effort, astonishment and long periods of time can be taken more slowly. Meaningful and emotional passages tend to be taken at a slower pace. A phrase which contains several ideas might also be taken more slowly and deliberately than one with a simple idea.

A faster pace can be achieved by shortening vowels and continuant consonants and shortening the space between words. Quick, easy, little, ordinary things can be taken more rapidly. An increase in pace can also be used to build to a climax.

Pace is affected by the distribution of stresses in a phrase. Lighter stressing and a more rhythmical distribution of stresses can be taken at a swifter pace.

Tempo or Rate

Tempo is the overall rate, or time signature, of the writing. Pace will fluctuate considerably within the limits of the tempo used by the speaker.

Pitch

Pitch is the specific level of highness or lowness in a speech note. A higher pitch is often used for lighter and happier thoughts. A lower pitch is often used for sombre and sad thoughts.

Inflection

Inflection refers to the rise and fall in pitch of the voice during speech. As the voice rises and falls it tends to form patterns or tunes. The two most commonly heard tunes in Received Pronunciation (R.P.) are called Falling Tune and Rising Tune.

1. Falling Tune

This is a simple falling pattern where the stressed syllables descend from a higher pitch to a lower one. It tends to be used for:

Complete statements

Commands

Agreement

Aggression

Strong emotion

Questions not requiring a 'yes' or 'no' answer

End of breath-groups

Try these examples:

We are fortunate to have John Smith spending the day with us.
Put that on the table.
Why do you want to go back there?

2. Rising Tune

This is also a pattern of descending stressed syllables, but there is a rise of pitch on the last syllable. It tends to be used for:

Doubt

Anxiety

Surprise

Pleading

Threats

Incomplete statements

Questions requiring a 'yes' or 'no' answer

The end of a single sense-group within a larger breath-group

Try these examples:
I'm not too sure about that one.
Please don't leave me now.
Would you like to come to the football match?

Inflection reflects our personality, our thoughts and our feelings. Flexible use of inflection will therefore reveal subtle changes in our moods.

Use of inflection must be unconscious or speech becomes stilted. The speaker should focus on communicating meaning and mood to avoid artificiality.

Tone Colour

Tone colour refers to the variation of light and shade in the voice. It is the result of various tensions and relaxations in the resonators and other allied muscles but is prompted by the imagination. The quality of tone therefore alters according to the mood, which helps the listener to recognise the mood of the speaker regardless of the words spoken.

In performance, the tone colour should reflect the mood of the prose or verse, but this must be sincerely imagined or it will sound false.

INTENSITY

Fluctuations in intensity indicate tension and relaxation according to the prevailing mood. A performer should avoid giving a whole performance at a high pitch of intensity as it is too tiring for both the performer and audience and the value of contrast would be lost.

*   *   *   *   *   *   *   *

Now think about when and why you use these features in the performance of your verse and prose. Be prepared to give the examiner specific examples.

Grade Six – Bronze Medal

Questions will be based on the following:

- *The story and characters of the book from which the prose selection has been taken*

- *Breathing, voice production, resonance and projection.*

The candidate must be prepared to discuss with the examiner any aspect of theory specified for previous grades.
(Page 30 *Specifications for Graded Examinations*)

BREATHING

'Breath is fundamental to life. It is also fundamental to producing voice. Because breathing is an involuntary activity, we seldom give it a thought unless it is difficult or painful. But if we hear that our voice is too soft, fades away or won't carry, we need to consider how we breathe.'

From *More Care for Your Voice* by the Voice Care Network UK.

There are a number of bones and muscles involved in the breathing process.

Bones

The spine is made up of a series of vertebrae. The twelve pairs of 'dorsal vertebrae' curve around to the front of the chest forming the rib cage. Seven pairs join with the sternum. Three pairs join with the seventh and two pairs are 'floating'. You can feel the definition of the ribs with your fingers.

Muscles

The Intercostal Muscles are situated between the ribs (inter = between, costal = ribs).

The Diaphragm is a dome shaped muscle dividing the chest and the abdomen. It is attached to the lower edges of the rib cage, the point of the sternum and, at the back, the vertebrae.

The Abdominal Muscles form part of the abdominal cavity and help to control the movement of the diaphragm.

Breathing In

When you decide to speak, a message is sent from the brain to the muscles. The intercostals contract and move the ribs slightly upwards and outwards. The diaphragm, which is attached to the ribs, moves in response to this action, flattening out. This creates more space inside the chest, giving the lungs room to expand. As the lungs expand, the air pressure reduces. Air immediately flows in through the nose or mouth in order to equalise the pressure. The abdominal muscles release.

Breathing Out

We then exhale. The muscles converge simultaneously to support the release of the breath. The abdominal muscles contract, the diaphragm rises and the rib cage returns to its original position through the movement of the intercostals. Air flows out through the nose and mouth, powered by the abdominal muscles.

Support

Your teacher may have given you a direction to 'support your voice'. This means having just the right amount of pressure from the abdominal muscles to create just the right amount of breath force for the sound you want to use. For example, if you want to project your voice across a large space then you will need a more consistent pressure from the abdominal muscles.

Breathing exercises will help you with this process. When you practise a breathing exercise, place your hands on your lower abdomen and centre your attention there. This will help the abdominal muscles to release on the in-breath and contract on the out-breath. Taking breath from your 'centre' will also help you to relax and release the sound more freely and easily.

Avoid...

Clavicular Breathing. This means moving the ribs upwards but not outwards when breathing in, holding air in the upper lungs and raising the shoulders. This sometimes happens when the body is tense, putting strain on the vocal folds. Make sure that your spine is lengthened, and your shoulders, neck and jaw are free from tension.

VOICE PRODUCTION

'Voice begins with an impulse from the brain. It is stimulated by an intention to speak or sing.

Two elements produce voice – a flow of air and vibration.

The air flows from breath. Air is taken in through the mouth or nose, passes down the trachea (or wind-pipe) and into the lungs. It is drawn there by contraction of the dome-like diaphragm. As the diaphragm relaxes, the abdominal muscles work to return breath up the trachea.

The larynx (or voice box) is located in the upper part of the trachea. Its primary biological function is to serve as a protective valve for the air-way. When we use our voice, we close two bands of muscular tissue in the larynx – the vocal folds (or cords) – across the air flow. The out-breath causes the edges of the folds to vibrate, generating sound, in a manner similar to that of air escaping from the neck of a balloon as it deflates. The edges of the folds are quite short – roughly 15-20 mm – and their vibration is extremely rapid. Depending on age, sex, health and the note pitched, the vocal folds may open and close between 60 and 1000 times per second.'

From *More Care for Your Voice* by the Voice Care
Network UK.

Figure 1
The Larynx (from the side)

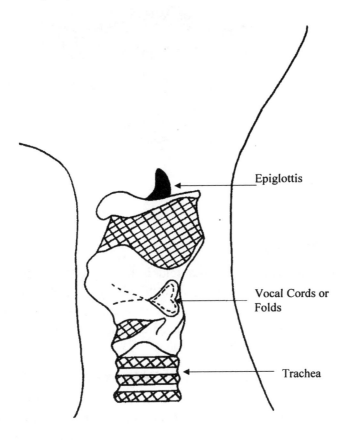

Figure 2
The Larynx (from above)

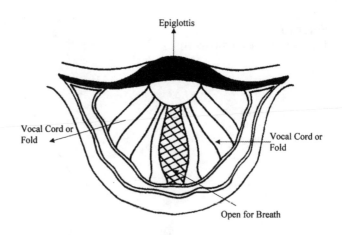

RESONANCE

The note created in the vocal folds is then carried by the breath through various hollow spaces: the **pharynx** or pharyngeal resonator, the **mouth** or oral resonator and the **nose** or nasal resonator. The note is strengthened, amplified and given texture as it travels through these spaces.

The Pharynx (Pharyngeal Resonator)

This is the long muscular tube which extends upwards from the larynx, ending at the back part of the oral and nasal cavities. It is the first resonating space through which the note must pass on its way to the mouth and nose.

The pharynx can change its shape and size which affects the quality of the sound produced. It increases in size during a yawn and decreases in size when the throat or neck is tense.

Try this:

> Hold a yawn in your throat and count 'one, two, three' at the same time. You will hear a sound with too much pharyngeal resonance.

The Mouth (Oral Resonator)

The lower jaw forms the floor of the oral resonator and is attached to the facial bones by hinge joints.

The tongue lies on the floor of the oral resonator, rooted in the front wall of the pharynx. It is capable of intricate and rapid movements. The movement is centred in different areas: the tip (point of the tongue), the blade (underneath the upper tooth ridge), the front (underneath the hard palate), the centre (partly underneath the hard palate and partly underneath the soft palate) and the back (underneath the soft palate).

The lips form the exit of the oral resonator at the free edges of the mouth and grip, direct and shape the breath stream.

The hard palate is an arched bone structure, separating the oral cavity from the nasal cavities, forming the roof of the mouth.

The soft palate forms the back third of the roof of the mouth, continuing from the curve of the hard palate. The back edge is free and can move up and down. Its movement controls the flow of air through the nose or mouth, like a trap door. When breathing naturally through the nose, the soft palate is relaxed and droops down into the mouth, which leaves the passage to the nose free. When there is an impulse to speak, the soft palate contracts upwards, blocking the passage to the nose, so that the air and sound flows through the mouth.

Try this:

> Allow your lower jaw to drop at its most natural point and use a mirror to look through to the back of the mouth. If you

breathe through your nose and out through your mouth with your mouth still open then you will see the action of the soft palate.

*   *   *   *   *   *   *

Breath carries the sound from the pharynx into the mouth. If the breath force is strong enough the sound will bounce off the hard palate and out through the lips. This is called *forward resonance*.

If the breath force is too weak to reach the hard palate, it may pitch onto the soft palate, which will make the sound difficult to project.

The mouth is capable of assuming a wide range of sizes and shapes because of the movement of the tongue, lips, jaw and soft palate. However, there needs to be space inside the mouth to create an appropriate amount of oral resonance.

Try this:

Say the long vowel sound 'ah' with your lower jaw dropped at its most natural point. Continue saying the sound and raise your lower jaw slowly. As the lower jaw comes up, the lips will move closer together and the tongue might move towards the hard palate. You will hear a sound without much oral resonance.

The Nose (Nasal Resonator)

There are two types of nasal resonance:

- When the vibrating column of air passes directly through the open soft palate to the nasal cavity. In English this only happens on three sounds – 'm', 'n' and 'ng'.

- When the vibrating column of air does not pass directly into the nasal cavity, but instead pitches

onto the hard palate just behind the upper teeth,
and the sound vibrations are carried through the
bones of the hard palate to the nasal cavities.
This type of nasal resonance can be heard in
vowel sounds.

To produce the first type of nasal resonance the soft palate must
be in good working order and to produce the second type of
nasal resonance there must be forward resonance (the breath
force is strong enough to bounce the sound off the hard palate).

If the speaker has a cold and the nasal cavities are blocked
then there won't be any nasal resonance. If the soft palate
doesn't close properly then too much nasal resonance will
leak into the sound.

Try this:
Say 'mum', 'nose' and 'sing'. Repeat the words but this
time hold your nose. You should hear 'bub', 'dose' and 'sig'
because there isn't any nasal resonance.

Balancing Resonance

Good resonance depends upon achieving a balance of vibration
from the pharynx, mouth and nose. The quality of the sound will
be affected if there is too much resonance from just one of the
resonators.

Exercises provided by your teacher will help you to find
this balance. When you practise your exercises, make sure
that your spine is lengthened, your shoulders, neck and jaw are
free from tension, there is space inside your mouth and an
adequate breath force to bring the sound forward. It is
important that you try not to think about all of this when you
are speaking or performing. You must practice your exercises
so that it comes to you naturally.

The quality of sound will also be affected if the resonators
are unhealthy (e.g. if you have a cold or sore throat).

Unfortunately there is little you can do to counteract the effects of illness on the quality of the sound.

Figure 3

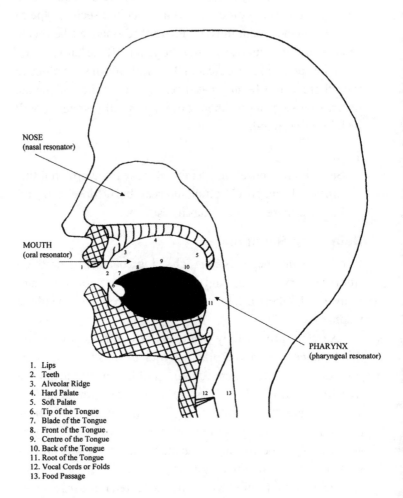

NOSE
(nasal resonator)

MOUTH
(oral resonator)

PHARYNX
(pharyngeal resonator)

1. Lips
2. Teeth
3. Alveolar Ridge
4. Hard Palate
5. Soft Palate
6. Tip of the Tongue
7. Blade of the Tongue
8. Front of the Tongue
9. Centre of the Tongue
10. Back of the Tongue
11. Root of the Tongue
12. Vocal Cords or Folds
13. Food Passage

Head and Chest Resonance

You may also feel vibrations from higher notes in your head and vibrations from lower notes in your chest when you speak, which are sometimes called head resonance and chest resonance. However, the head and chest are not official resonators as the vibrations come from sound waves produced by pharyngeal, oral and nasal resonance. For this reason, head and chest resonance are sometimes referred to as secondary resonance.

PROJECTION

Projection involves:

1. AUDIBILITY

- Strong, secure breath

  (breath supported by the abdominal, diaphragmatic and intercostal muscles, and, released freely and easily)

- Forward placement of resonance

  (air and sound brought forward in the mouth, using the hard palate as a sounding board)

2. INTELLIGIBILITY

- Clarity of speech

  (tongue and lip muscularity; precise articulation)

- Appropriate emphasis and modulation

  (varying use of stress, volume, pace, pitch, inflection, tone colour and pausing, according to the thought and emotion being expressed)

3. MENTAL PROJECTION

- Engagement with the audience in order to communicate across the divide

Grade Seven – Silver Medal

The candidate may be asked about any or all of the following:

- *The story and characters of the book from which the prose selection has been taken*

- *Metre and rhythm (iambic, anapaestic, dactylic and spondaic rhythms). Definitions must be illustrated with examples from the chosen pieces where possible*

- *Specific verse forms (blank verse, free verse and sonnet form)*

- *Figures of speech (alliteration, assonance, onomatopoeia, antithesis, pun, simile, metaphor). Definitions must be illustrated with examples from the chosen pieces where possible.*

The candidate must be prepared to discuss with the examiner any aspect of theory specified for previous grades.

(Page 32 *Specifications for Graded Examinations*)

METRE AND RHYTHM

English speech rhythm is formed by a combination of weak and strong stresses. English verse rhythm depends upon the arrangement of these stresses into patterns. When that pattern is regular and repeated it is called metre.

One bar or unit of a metrical form is called a 'foot', derived from dancing in Ancient Greece when the foot was raised and set down on the stressed beat of a musical bar.

A metric line is named according to the number of feet within it:

Monometer	=	one foot to a line
Dimeter	=	two feet to a line
Trimeter	=	three feet to a line
Tetrameter	=	four feet to a line
Pentameter	=	five feet to a line
Hexameter	=	six feet to a line
Heptameter	=	seven feet to a line
Octometer	=	eight feet to a line

A metric line is also named according to the type of rhythm within the unit or bar. In English verse there are two main types: Falling Rhythm and Rising Rhythm.

RISING RHYTHM

Iambus (an iambic foot)

An iambic foot consists of an unstressed followed by a stressed syllable.

weak **strong** | weak **strong** | weak **strong** | weak **strong** | weak **strong** | (iambic pentameter)

de **dum**, de **dum**, de **dum**, de **dum**, de **dum** (iambic pentameter)

It comes from the Greek word meaning 'to hurl' or 'to throw', used when writers of satire hurled their verse, like a weapon, at their enemies. The rhythm resembles the beating of a human heart and is very close to natural speech patterns. Although we may not be aware of it, everyday conversation frequently falls into an iambic rhythm.

I hope you take the book with you to school.

I **hope** | you **take** | the **book** | with **you** | to **school** |
The ticket isn't valid for today.

The **tick** | et **is** | n't **val** | id **for** | to**day** |

This is one reason why Elizabethan dramatists, who were heavily influenced by the metrical forms adopted by the Greek and Latin poets of antiquity, were attracted to it. The forward drive of the iambus also makes it ideal for ongoing narrative.

Romeo speaks in iambic pentameter as he waits below Juliet's window in *Romeo and Juliet*.

But soft! What light through yonder window breaks?

But **soft!** | What **light** | through **yon** | der **win** | dow **breaks?** |

Notice how the metrical structure of the line gives emphasis to the words 'soft', 'light' and 'breaks'.

Anapaest (an anapaestic foot)

An anapaestic foot consists of two unstressed syllables followed by a stressed syllable.

de de **dum** | de de **dum** | de de **dum** | de de **dum** | de de **dum** |

This creates a rapid effect, driving the line of the verse forward, which mirrors the movement in Lord Byron's *The Destruction of Sennacherib*.

The Assyrian came down like the wolf on the fold;
And his cohorts were gleaming in purple and gold:

The A**ssyr** | ian came **down** | like the **wolf** | on the **fold;** |
And his **co** | horts were **gleam** | ing in **pur** | ple and **gold:** |

FALLING RHYTHM

Trochee (a trochaic foot)

A trochaic foot consists of a stressed syllable followed by an unstressed syllable.

dum de | **dum** de | **dum** de | **dum** de | **dum** de |
Never | **Nev**er | **Nev**er | **Nev**er | **Nev**er |

King Lear's response upon discovering his daughter Cordelia dead, is captured in the mournful, falling tone of the metre.

Shakespeare often uses a trochee at the start of an iambic line, which emphasises the meaning of the first word, for example:

Weary with toil, I haste me to my bed, (Sonnet 27)

Weary | with **toil**, | I **haste** | me **to** | my **bed**, |

Dactyl (a dactylic foot)

A dactylic foot consists of a stressed syllable followed by two unstressed syllables.

dum de de | **dum** de de | **dum** de de | **dum** de de | **dum** de de |

In the following line from *Hamlet* the metre places stress on the word 'that', highlighting the reflective nature of the speech and drawing our attention to the 'question'. The use of two lighter syllables in the fourth foot rapidly moves the line forward to 'question'.

To be, or not to be, that is the question

To **be**, | or **not** | to **be**, | **that** is the | **quest**ion |

OTHER RHYTHMS

Spondee (a spondaic foot)

A spondaic foot consists of two successive syllables with equal weight.

| **dum dum** |

It is usually used in the middle or end of a line for extra emphasis. An example can be found in *The Rime of the Ancient Mariner* by Samuel Taylor Coleridge.

Alone, alone, **all, all** alone,
Alone on a wide, wide sea!

BLENDING OF RHYTHMS

A succession of lines consisting of the same kind of metrical rhythm can be monotonous. Many poets have therefore combined different rhythms to create interest. Sometimes a poem can pass from rising to falling rhythm and back again. A change in rhythm can bring a change in the meaning or mood; equally, a change in the meaning or mood can bring a change in the rhythm.

SCANSION

To 'scan' a piece of verse is to go through it line by line, analysing the number of feet and marking the weak and strong stresses. Whilst it is not necessary to scan poems or speeches in detail, it is absolutely imperative that you have a firm grasp of the ways in which poetic structure links with thought and emotion. You must become a detective, searching out the clues within verse structure that bring the text to life. An understanding of metrical patterning can often provide the key to a passage that might at first seem difficult to comprehend. If you know where the stresses fall in a given speech you will find it easier to locate the sense!

It is important that the rules of poetic form are not isolated from thought and emotion. Working with the rhythm and metre must be connected to feeling and impulse otherwise you will end up speaking the metre but not the sense.

SPECIFIC VERSE FORMS

Blank Verse

Blank verse consists of a succession of unrhymed iambic pentameters (five iambic feet to a line). It creates a sense of simplicity and directness, perfect for character speech and dramatic performance. Shakespeare even mentions the term in *Hamlet*.

Hamlet: The lady shall say her mind freely, or the
                 Blank verse shall halt for it.

Sometimes the occasional trochee, anapaest, dactyl or spondee
is added, in order to create variety (please refer to 'Blending of
Rhythms').

Hermione's trial speech in *The Winter's Tale* is in blank
verse but includes a metrical change in the fifth line, which
strengthens her sense of innocence.

Hermione: Since what I am to say, must be but that
                 Which contradicts my accusation, and
                 The testimony on my part, no other
                 But what comes from myself, it shall
                                           scarce boot me
                 To say 'not guilty';

Free Verse

It is a common misapprehension that free verse is without form.
Free verse possesses a structure but it is much more open and
less bound by classical rules.

Free verse is not necessarily confined to a specific
metrical law but uses a rhythm most suitable for the
expression of a particular thought and emotion. For example,
if the thought or emotion is more stately then the rhythm will
move more slowly on; if the thought or emotion is lighter then
the rhythm will gallop along.

A unit is not therefore a foot or a line, but a stanza or even
the whole poem itself.

Rhyme can be included in free verse but is usually a
necessary part of the thought and/or emotion.

Free verse came into its own in the early twentieth century
with the modernist movement. TS Eliot's *Love Song of J.
Alfred Prufrock* is a particular example.

Let us go then, you and I,
When the evening is spread out against the sky
Like a patient etherised upon a table;

Or Walt Whitman's *Out of the Cradle Endlessly Rocking*
taken from *Leaves of Grass*.

Till of a sudden,
May-be kill'd, unknown to her mate,
One forenoon the she-bird crouch'd not on the nest,
Nor return'd that afternoon, nor the next,
Nor ever appear'd again.

And thenceforward, all summer, in the sound of
                                    the sea,
And at night, under the full of the moon, in calmer
                                    weather,
Over the hoarse surging of the sea,
Or flitting from brier to brier by day,
I saw, I heard at intervals, the remaining one, the
                                    he-bird
The solitary guest from Alabama.

Sonnet Form

The Petrarchan or Italian Sonnet

The sonnet form is of Italian origin dating back to the
Renaissance and was used by both Petrarch and Dante. The
Petrarchan Sonnet consists of fourteen lines divided into an
octave and a sestet.

- The octave is made up of two quatrains (a
  quatrain is a set of four lines)

- The sestet is composed of two tercets (or sets of
  three lines)

When the sonnet is written in Italian the rhyming scheme is limited. In the octave only two rhymes are the norm: *abba abba*. Three pairs of rhymes are found in the tercet: *cde cde*.

The subject consists of one idea which is stated, often in universal terms, boldly in the first quatrain and developed in the second. A pause then follows. In each of the two tercets the subject is again considered but this time it tends to be particularised. Finally it is brought to a definite and forceful close.

The Petrarchan Sonnet was introduced from Italy into England by Sir Thomas Wyatt and developed by Henry Howard, Earl of Surrey. Difficulties were encountered. Italian is a musical and flexible language, far more so than English, and in order to accommodate the language change extra rhymes had to be incorporated. A second change in the form was the rearrangement of the sestet in a variety of ways: sometimes the change would be in the rhyming scheme which was altered to *cd cd cd* with the sense continued in the series of three couplets (a set of two lines) instead of spread over two tercets. In England the form became more flexible than in Italy.

An example of the English development of the Petrarchan Sonnet is William Wordsworth's *Upon Westminster Bridge.*

Earth has not anything to show more fair:
Dull would he be of soul who could pass by
A sight so touching in its majesty:
This city now doth, like a garment, wear
The beauty of the morning; silent, bare,
Ships, towers, domes, theatres, and temples lie
Open unto the fields, and to the sky:
All bright and glittering in the smokeless air.
Never did sun more beautifully steep
In his first splendour, valley, rock, or hill:
Ne'er saw I, never felt, a calm so deep!

The river glideth at his own sweet will:
Dear God! The very houses seem asleep;
And all that mighty heart is lying still.

The Shakespearean Sonnet

William Shakespeare departed from the tightly interlaced model of the Petrarchan sonnet and in its place he used a form which, although it still consists of an octave and a sestet with a pause between the two, breaks into different shapes:

- The octave is divided into two quatrains, made distinct by the rhyme scheme which runs: *abab cdcd*

- The sestet consists of a quatrain, *efef*, and a final couplet, *gg*

This pattern allows Shakespeare:

- To present an argument in the octave

- To recognise either a development or a contradiction of this in the first four lines of the sestet

- To make a strong concluding statement in the couplet.

This is particularly evident in Sonnet 97.

How like a winter hath my absence been
From thee, the pleasure of the fleeting year!
What freezings have I felt, what dark days seen,
What old December's bareness everywhere!
And yet this time removed was summer's time,
The teeming autumn big with rich increase
Bearing the wanton burden of the prime,
Like widowed wombs after their lords' decease:
Yet this abundant issue seemed to me

But hope of orphans, and unfathered fruit;
For summer and his pleasures wait on thee,
And thou away, the very birds are mute;
Or if they sing, 'tis with so dull a cheer
That leaves look pale, dreading the winter's near.

FIGURES OF SPEECH

A figure of speech is a non-literal expression or one which uses a particular pattern of words for emphasis. Such features are found more commonly in verse than prose, though some are used quite regularly in everyday speech without being recognised for what they are.

Alliteration

Alliteration is the repetition of an initial consonant. This can produce a striking effect when the poem is spoken aloud. One example of the repetition of the crisp 'k' sound is found in the opening line of TS Eliot's *The Journey of the Magi*.

A cold coming we had of it...

Leonard Clark uses the liquid 'l' sound for a smoother effect in *Singing in the Streets*.

Firelight, lamplight, the little lame cat...

Assonance

Assonance, less commonly used than alliteration, is the repetition of a vowel sound, and again it is particularly noticeable when the lines are spoken. The short 'i' is used in John Fuller's *Tides*, which adds to the light, smooth movement of the verse.

It's time to go, but still we sit
Lingering in our summer
Like idle fingers,
Like fingers in the sand.

The opening lines of Coleridge's *Kubla Khan* provide a good example of alliteration and assonance combined.

> In Xanadu did Kubla Khan
> A stately pleasure dome decree:
> Where Alph, the sacred river, ran
> Through caverns measureless to man
> Down to a sunless sea.

Onomatopoeia

Onomatopoeia is another device which makes particular use of sounds, as it refers to those words that make a sound similar to their meaning when spoken aloud. Among the simplest are 'pop' and 'hiss'. There are relatively few words which really fulfil this criteria but in poetry there is often an onomatopoeic quality to phrases which enhance the meaning when spoken. One example is from Wilfrid Owen's *Anthem for Doomed Youth*.

> The stuttering rifles' rapid rattle

Brian Lee's *Night Music* also concentrates on sound.

> A door clicks; and swishes open, on its own...
> Milk bottles tinkle on a step. A window shrieks
> Upwards; the bath-tap whispers as it leaks...

Antithesis

Antithesis occurs when a word, phrase or idea is set in opposition to another, resulting in a strong contrast or ambiguity which can often surprise or shock. It is quite a dramatic device and often used by Shakespeare. A striking example of antitheses can be seen in one of Romeo's speeches from the first scene of *Romeo and Juliet*.

> Here's much to do with hate, but more with love.
> Why then, O brawling love! O loving hate

O anything, of nothing first create!
O heavy lightness! Serious vanity!
Mis-shapen chaos of well-seeming forms!
Feather of lead, bright smoke, cold fire, sick health!
Still-waking sleep, that is not what it is!

Pun

A pun plays not with the sound but with the meanings of words. It uses a word which has two different meanings both of which are relevant in the context. This ambiguity is often humorous, as in Richard Edwards' poem *Waterway Robbery*, which is about a carp who has to pay money to the more dominant pike.

'Thank goodness,' the carp thought,
'That rivers have banks!'

Simile

A simile is one of the most commonly used figures of speech, likening one thing to another thing. One simple and well-known example is the opening line of Robert Burns' poem –

My love is like a red, red rose.

A more unusual simile is found in Berlie Docherty's *Quieter than Snow*, where she writes;

Silence hung in the yard like sheets.

You can always recognise a simile by the use of the words 'like' or 'as'.

Metaphor

A metaphor is more powerful than a simile as it turns one thing into something else. A clear example comes in Shakespeare's *Othello*, when Iago speaks:

O, beware, my lord, of jealousy;
It is the green-eyed monster, which doth mock
The meat it feeds on.

Some metaphors are extended through a whole piece of writing. In Andrew Young's poem *Hard Frost*, the frost is seen as an army and the image is sustained through the whole poem.

Personification

Personification is where inanimate things are endowed with human qualities. In *Ode to the West Wind* Shelley addresses the west wind as if it is a person. Time is personified in Shakespeare's sonnets, for example –

And nothing 'gainst time's scythe can make defence
Save breed to brave him, when he takes thee hence.

(Sonnet XII)

Devouring time, blunt thou the lion's paws,
And make the earth devour her own sweet brood;

Yet do thy worst, old Time, despite thy wrong,
My love shall in my verse ever live young.

(Sonnet XIX)

*   *   *   *   *   *   *

Now look for examples of these features in your chosen verse. Be prepared to talk through these examples with the examiner.

Grade Eight – Gold Medal

Questions will be based on the following:

- *The story and characters of the book from which the prose selection has been taken and/ or play from which the Shakespeare selection has been taken*

- *The writers' biographical details and the social/historical context of their writing.*

The candidate must be prepared to discuss with the examiner any aspect of theory specified for previous grades.
(Page 33 *Specifications for Graded Examinations*)

The following pages provide information on the writers listed in the Specifications.

John Burnside

T S Eliot

Lawrence Ferlinghetti

Philip Larkin

Edna St Vincent Millay

Pablo Neruda

Muriel Stuart

Jonathan Swift

Isabel Allende

Peter Carey

George Eliot

Henry James

Bernard MacLaverty

Rohinton Mistry

Dorothy Parker

Bram Stoker

William Shakespeare

John Burnside

John Burnside was born in Dunfermline in 1955, but his family moved south to Corby in Lancashire when he was eleven. He studied English and European Languages at Cambridge College of Art and Technology and after graduation he took various temporary jobs, including being a peanut fryer, before deciding to train as a teacher. There followed two years in the Civil Service before he went into computing, designing software. He lived in Surrey for a number of years and only returned to his native Scotland in 1996 when he became a full-time writer. He now lives in Fife and is a lecturer in Creative Writing at St. Andrew's University.

His first volume of poetry, *The Hoop*, appeared in 1988, followed by several others, including *The Asylum Dance*, which won the 2001 Whitbread Poetry Award. His latest book is *The Light Trap*, which was published in 2002.

Burnside also writes fiction, darker in tone than most of his poetry, but reflecting similar themes. His first novel, *The Dumb House,* which came out in 1997, is a sinister story of children involved in a language experiment. A youthful obsession with Elvis Presley is reflected in his short story collection *Burning Elvis*. *Living Nowhere*, his most recent novel, explores themes of immigration and exile. The first part is set in 1970s Corby and examines the empty life of a Scottish family among the town's grim steel mills. Francis, the main character, walks away when his best friend is murdered and spends seventeen years 'in exile' trying to find some meaning in his life. When he finally returns home he discovers that what he had been searching for was perhaps there all the time.

The poems in *The Asylum Dance* also focus on the concept of home and being away from home. Home is safe, a 'port', but there is always the lure of the unfamiliar world outside. The fishermen of the Scottish coast are a recurring image – men who regularly explore the world beyond but who return thankfully each time to their home port.

In all his work Burnside examines the relationship between man and the natural world, pursuing his quest for what he calls 'the spirit', which can take us outside the time and place which we inhabit. His natural world is that of the Scottish countryside and coast. Poems like *Geese* and *Kestrel* recall some of Ted Hughes' early writing, where nature provides a metaphor for human endeavour. Burnside does not make much use of metaphor however; his style is spare and direct, the images sharp, and varied rhythms strongly felt.

Burnside has said that he sees poetry 'as a form of alchemy', in which man can be guided, through a contact with nature, to a more spiritual understanding. In this way his poetry can be seen as a quest which is not yet resolved:

> forgive me
>> being not the man I seem
> not lost or found
>> but somewhere in between.

T S Eliot

T S Eliot has probably had more influence than any other writer on the development of English poetry in the twentieth century, yet he lived his first twenty-five years in the United States.

He was born in September 1888 in St Louis, Missouri, the youngest of six children who, between his mother and four sisters, was somewhat cosseted. The family were committed Unitarians, and had a strong sense of duty and responsibility. His father, however, had eschewed the ministry to become a successful businessman.

Eliot went to a local school and then to the Smith Academy. Because he suffered from a congenital hernia he was barred from many physical activities and was known as a quiet, bookish boy who wrote verse, easily adopting the style of whichever poet he was reading.

In 1905 he left home for the first time to spend a year at Milton Academy in Boston as a preparation for entering Harvard University, which he did the following year. He took his AB (US equivalent of a British BA) in three years instead of the usual four and then read for an MA in English Literature. Contemporaries recalled him as being a bit of a recluse but also something of a dandy!

During this time he was writing consistently and in the notebooks he kept there are early drafts of *Portrait of a Lady* and *Preludes*. In these it is possible already to see his concern with urban drabness and squalor which feature in so many of his early published poems together with a sense of withdrawal.

Eliot made his first trip to Europe in October 1910, spending a year in Paris where he was lonely but stimulated by the intellectual climate which was more forward-looking than that he had encountered in the States. He returned to Harvard to study philosophy and in 1914 the University offered him a travelling fellowship to pursue his work in Britain. Arriving in London, he met with fellow American poet Ezra Pound, who was to become his closest literary friend. It was partly through Pound's efforts that *Preludes*, *Rhapsody on a Windy Night* and *The Love Song of J. Alfred Prufrock* were published in literary magazines. Then the First World War broke out.

For Eliot, of more immediate significance than the war, was his sudden marriage in 1915 to Vivien Haigh-Wood. She appeared a vivacious and witty character but was subject to quick changes of mood and had a history of illness. Quite soon it became clear to Eliot that the marriage was a failure physically and he found it increasingly difficult to cope with Vivien's unstable personality. However, as a married man, Eliot needed to earn some money. He began teaching (young male teachers had virtually disappeared during the war) and later obtained work in Lloyds' bank. Life in London must have been strange for the young American with most of his British contemporaries away fighting and dying. The impact of the war can be seen in *The Waste Land* which he began just after the end of hostilities under the title of *He Do the Police in Different Voices.*

The Waste Land was published in 1922 and was to become the single most influential poem in twentieth-century literature. Other works followed, including *Sweeney Agonistes*, *The Hollow Men* and *Ash Wednesday*. His reputation grew and he had an offer of more congenial employment than that found working in the bank – director of the publishing firm Faber and Gwyer (later to become Faber & Faber). As an editor he became responsible for publishing most of the notable poets of the time. He was also writing perceptive critical essays for the *Times Literary Supplement* and other literary magazines.

1927 saw two significant happenings in Eliot's life. He was confirmed as a member of the Church of England and he became a British citizen. These events seemed to provide him with a stability and assurance that he had hitherto lacked and which his innate sense of order and duty seemed to need. From this time his work underwent a change of approach – the 'modernist' poet became increasingly conservative and a member of the establishment.

In 1932 Eliot became Norton Professor at Harvard. The lectures he gave there were subsequently published as *The Use of Poetry and the Use of Criticism*. On his return to London he finally separated from Vivien, ending a stressful marriage, with Vivien's mental state becoming increasingly unstable. She was eventually confined to a mental hospital where she died in 1947.

1935 saw a new success for Eliot which also confirmed his status as a member of the establishment. His verse drama

Murder in the Cathedral was performed in Canterbury Cathedral to great acclaim. There was some revival of interest in verse dramas at the time. Christopher Fry and John Masefield were writers who also tried their hands at this genre with varying success. Eliot followed his first play with several others over the next twelve years, the most successful, in box-office terms, being *The Cocktail Party*. Unlike *Murder in the Cathedral* these were aimed at the commercial theatre and had contemporary settings.

In 1939 came the Second World War. Eliot, still at Faber's, and having just produced the *Book of Practical Cats*, eventually moved to Surrey for the duration. His most complex work, *The Four Quartets*, was written and published in 1943. It is a sign of his standing that, even with war-time paper shortages, 17,000 copies of *Little Giddings* (the last part of the sequence) were printed. His reputation was high, cemented by articles and lectures, and after the war his position was recognised by the award, in 1948, of both the Order of Merit and the Nobel Prize for Literature.

Ten years after Vivien's death, and at the age of sixty-eight, Eliot married his thirty-year old secretary, Valerie Fletcher, and this relationship brought him the happiness he had never had before. The marriage lasted until Eliot's death in January 1965. His ashes were scattered in the churchyard at East Coker, from which village his ancestors had supposedly set out to make a new life in America and which Eliot had used as inspiration for the second section of *The Four Quartets*. His memorial stone in the churchyard includes lines from the poem *East Coker*:

In my beginning is my end. –
In my end is my beginning.

Eliot's work has been the subject of much scholarly appraisal, and he has the reputation of being a 'difficult' writer. Certainly his later work is dense, intense and packed with allusions not easy to follow. Nonetheless, the rhythms and sound patterns of the carefully chosen words carry the reader forward and a certain sensual appreciation can be achieved without resort to in-depth analysis of deeper levels of meaning. His earlier poetry is more easily accessible, supported by powerful rhythms.

Preludes and *The Love Song of J Alfred Prufrock* have many features we have come to associate with Eliot. The title of the second is humorous, suggesting the pretensions of the social climber. The approach is that of the detached, rather cynical observer of contemporary life. Eliot was never a full-time writer and his daily office routine brought him into contact with all the depressing realities of city drudgery:

> The burnt-out ends of smoky days...

> The faint stale smells of beer
> From the sawdust-trampled street
> With all its muddy feet that press
> To early coffee stands.

'The yellow fog that rubs its back upon the window panes', not only conjures up the reality of London smog but also memories of the industrial city of St Louis. The light, free verse rhythms were new to English poetry and often echo the jazz rhythms of the popular music of the period which originated in the southern states of America.

The final form of *The Love Song of J Alfred Prufrock* was influenced by Ezra Pound, who urged Eliot to cut out some of the narrative, explanatory passages and so sharpen the impression that the images make on the reader. Pound began the 'Imagist' movement, which sought clarity of expression through the use of concentrated and juxtaposed images. He too, like Eliot, used the language of everyday speech. These were important features of the 'Modernist' school which dominated the post-war literary scene, where the conventions of nineteenth-century poetry were rejected. There was a sense of being cut off from the past by the terrible carnage of the First World War and a need for some new way to express the search for stability out of the chaos. This approach is a feature in Eliot's early poetry, the culmination of which was *The Waste Land*. The fragmentary structure reflects the disintegration that follows war and a lack of order which is disturbing:

> The river's tent is broken...
> But at my back in a cold blast I hear
> The rattle of the bones.

The meaning of *The Waste Land* has been much discussed and Eliot's own notes on the poem do not greatly help to explain his intentions. For the reader, the series of visual and auditory images combined with a skilful use of repetitions give an almost hallucinatory quality, but not a soporific one, to the poem. The writing moves from one rhythm to another with varying pictures, some very individual, others more universally representative in function.

Although it is not possible to examine Eliot's later work here, for the interested student it is worth looking at his last great poetic sequence *The Four Quartets*, written during the Second World War. Although the verse is much more austere and abstract in concept than *The Waste Land* there is greater acceptance of man's fate:

> We shall not cease from exploration
> And the end of all our exploring
> Will be to arrive where we started
> And know the place for the first time.

Lawrence Ferlinghetti

Born in March 1919 in Yonkers, New York, Ferlinghetti became a leading writer of the Beat Generation and is still an influential voice in American poetry.

His father, who died when Ferlinghetti was a baby, was an Italian immigrant who changed his name to Ferling; his son reverted to the original form of Ferlinghetti in 1954. After his father's death Ferlinghetti's mother became increasingly unstable and had to be confined to a mental hospital, leaving the young boy in the charge of an aunt, who took him to France for several years. He learnt to speak French before he could speak English.

He began writing poetry at boarding school and continued when he moved on to the University of North Carolina. His first degree was followed by a doctorate at the Sorbonne. His dissertation, entitled *The City as Symbol in Modern Poetry: In Search of a Metropolitan Tradition*, is an indication of how his interest in poetry was developing.

After service in the U.S. Navy during the Second World War, Ferlinghetti moved to San Francisco, taught French and, together with a colleague, started a magazine which they called *City Lights* after a Charlie Chaplin film. In 1953, to help with finances, they opened a book shop beneath the magazine offices. The 'City Lights Bookstore' was the first all-paperback shop in America and it quickly became a meeting place for writers and artists, a role it still has today. It is even featured on tourist itineraries.

Soon Ferlinghetti was publishing his own work and that of the like minded under the City Lights imprint. Most significant was the *Pocket Poets* series, aimed at publishing new writers at an affordable price. Among titles in the series was Allan Ginsberg's *Howl*, the publication of which led to Ferlinghetti being tried for obscenity. The case attracted huge publicity and it was held as a triumph for freedom of speech when Ferlinghetti was acquitted.

His own first collection of poems appeared in 1958, with the intriguing title of *A Coney Island of the Mind*, which rapidly became the most popular volume of poetry in the United States. Since then Ferlinghetti has produced more than thirty books of poetry, short experimental plays and two novels. His latest publication is *San Francisco Poems,* which came out in 2002. In recent years he has also achieved some acclaim as a painter.

In 1994 San Francisco named a street after Ferlinghetti and four years later he was given the title of 'Poet Laureate of San Francisco' in acknowledgement of his achievements.

Ferlinghetti has always been classed as one of the leading poets of the Beat Generation, though he has said that he does not consider himself a true Beat. The name Beat Generation was given to that group of young, anarchic writers who congregated at North Beach in the 1950s. They spoke out against the conservatism and materialism of the post-war period, were deeply concerned with social issues and strove for a voice that was non-elitist and direct. Leading writers of the group included Allan Ginsberg and Jack Kerouac. Ferlinghetti's work undoubtedly shows the characteristics of the Beat poets, but he is probably the most clearly political among them. His work has an instant appeal, using simple, direct language, a firm focus and a variety of free-verse patterns which points the juxtaposition of some unexpected images:

> Constantly risking absurdity
> > and death...

He prefers the language of everyday speech and the lively rhythms of jazz to make his poems accessible and relevant to his readers. The tone is often satirical, especially when describing the American urban lifestyle:

> I am singing about the downtrodden masses
> and the rich on their fat asses
>
> (*Blind Poet*)

The lack of punctuation and minimal use of capital letters is reminiscent of e.e.cummings, and like cummings, his verse seems to surge forward untrammelled by conventions.

In spite of his often gloomy views on modern life, his poetry overall is not depressing; he can see hope for a better future. This is very clear in *Wild Dreams of a New Beginning*, the opening line of which neatly parodies Henry Newbolt's *Vitae Lampada* –

> There's a desperate hush on the freeway tonight...

and builds a picture of life in the concrete city, which is then overtaken by a tidal wave, and so enforced to return to a more natural way of living. Light is a recurring image in his work, perhaps enhanced by his experiences as a painter. His volume *How to Paint Sunlight* contains many examples and poems on individual artists such as Monet, to whom light was of particular significance.

Today Ferlinghetti continues to run his book shop and to write a weekly column for the *San Francisco Chronicle*.

Philip Larkin

Philip Larkin, one of the most widely read of twentieth-century poets, was born in Coventry in 1922. His father, Sydney, was the City Treasurer and had a strong interest in language and literature (he would read Fowler's *Modern English Usage* for pleasure); he was also keen on jazz. Both these interests he passed on to his son.

Larkin went to the King Henry VIII School in Coventry and wrote his first poem there, aged sixteen, as a homework assignment. Until he was twenty-one he suffered with a serious stammer, which undoubtedly contributed to his reputation as a quiet, bookish boy. In 1940 he went up to St John's College, Oxford to read English. He failed his Army medical because of poor eye-sight so, unusually for a young man of that time, he had an uninterrupted three years of study and graduated with a first in 1943. While at Oxford he developed his interest in jazz as well as having a wide circle of literary friends, the closest of whom was Kingsley Amis. Their friendship was to be lifelong. Larkin's first published poem appeared in the magazine *The Listener* and several others featured in university magazines.

After graduation Larkin returned to his parents' home for a brief spell. He tried twice, and failed, to get into the Civil Service, and eventually got the job of Librarian in Wellington, Shropshire, where he was to stay for three years. He intended to become a novelist and had already begun work on *Jill*, which drew on his experiences of life in war-time Oxford. Being somewhat isolated away from home and friends did, he later admitted, 'create a raw state of mind that was very fruitful.' Several of his poems from this period appeared in the anthology *Poetry from Oxford in Wartime* and these were later included in his first individual volume, *The North Ship*, published in 1945. This was followed by the publication of *Jill* in 1946 and a year later, *A Girl in Winter*, his second novel in which he made use of his life as a librarian.

In 1947 he moved to Leicester to become Assistant Librarian at University College. Here he began to study part-time for his Library Association Examinations which he took and passed in 1949. At this time he met Monica Jones, a lecturer in English, with whom he had a lifelong affair. He began several novels but found himself unable to complete any of them, something his friend Kingsley Amis attributed to Larkin's deep fear of failure.

Larkin made another move in 1950 when he took the post of Sub-Librarian at Queen's University, Belfast, and here he began another fruitful period of writing. In 1951 he had *XX Poems* published privately and three years later his second volume *The Less Deceived* which was to form the foundation of his reputation as one of Britain's leading poets.

Larkin's final career move was made in 1955 when he was appointed Librarian at Hull University, where he was to remain for the rest of his life. He confessed to enjoying librarianship and had no desire to become a full-time writer. Hull suited him because he found it 'off the beaten track…a lonely place'. It was in Hull that he met the other two women with whom he had significant affairs, his fellow librarian, Maeve Brennan, and his secretary Betty Mackereth. But Larkin never married – the ties and demands of a monogamous relationship scared him and interfered with his need for solitude.

It was ten years after the appearance of *The Less Deceived* that Larkin's next volume of poetry was published. *The Whitsun Weddings* cemented his reputation. Some critics saw him as one of the leading figures of 'The Movement', a loosely-knit group of writers who had in common a rejection of modernist ideas and who used plain language and traditional verse forms to appeal to a wide readership.

In 1965 Larkin was awarded the Queen's Gold Medal for Poetry. He rejected the offer to become Poet Laureate after the death of his friend John Betjeman, as this for Larkin would have meant too much time in the public eye. His last book of verse, *High Windows*, came out in 1974, by which time he was beginning to feel he could no longer write. In an interview in 1982 he commented: 'I haven't given poetry up, but I rather think poetry has given me up.' He did however continue to be a leading figure on the literary scene. He produced a book of miscellaneous prose writings, *Required Writing*, in 1983 which won the W.H. Smith Literary Award. He also served as chairman of the judges for the Booker Prize, was a member of the literary panel of the Arts Council, and edited the popular *Oxford Book of Twentieth Century Verse*. He died of cancer in December 1985, having earlier in the year been elected a Companion of Honour.

In spite of Larkin's rather dour public persona and his nickname, 'the Hermit of Hull', his poetry has proved remarkably popular. His writing is usually direct and deals with ordinary characters in everyday situations, often in an urban setting. *Mr Bleaney*, one of his most anthologised pieces, creates, in unadorned language and with the use of a few carefully chosen details, the setting of the rented room and the personalities involved:

> This was Mr Bleaney's room. He stayed
> The whole time he was at the Bodies, till
> They moved him. Flowered curtains, thin and
> frayed...

> Bed, upright chair, sixty-watt bulb, no hook
> Behind the door, no room for books or bags.

As many of Larkin's poems do, *Mr Bleaney* moves from the particular scene to a wider view and so to a more universal significance. It also uses a traditional four-line stanza with ease and flexibility.

People and city-scapes are perhaps Larkin's most frequent subjects, but he also wrote about the natural world with real empathy. Animals in particular he would often see as victims of man's selfishness. There is the painful picture of the dying rabbit in *Myxomatosis* and in *At Grass* he shows sympathy for the old horses, who were forced to spend their youth being ridden round a race course for man's entertainment. It is only now that they

> stand at ease,
> Or gallop for what must be joy,
> And not a fieldglass sees them home.

Larkin is often thought of as having a pessimistic outlook and death is certainly a subject that constantly engages him. He admitted that he was afraid of dying, of 'endless extinction', and this threat is found in poems such as *An Arundel Tomb*, *The Building*, *Hospital Visits* and in his last poem *Aubade*, where he writes that

> the dread
> Of dying, and being dead,
> Flashes afresh to hold and horrify.

At the end however he can express a certain stoicism; the fact that life still goes on and 'Work has to be done.'

Throughout his career Larkin wrote with perception and sensitivity, but in a style that made his ideas readily accessible. He disliked the trend to make poetry difficult, influenced perhaps by his upbringing in the industrial midlands, which gave him an appreciation of the direct language of ordinary working people. He is said to have declared that 'deprivation is to me what daffodils are to Wordsworth'. Certainly life in the mid-twentieth century for the man on the street has been celebrated by him. Since his death his popularity has resulted in several television programmes on his life and work, a controversial biography by Andrew Motion, and Tom Courtney's one-man play *Pretending to be Me*. In life his personality often appeared unappealing, but his poetry continues to fascinate.

Edna St Vincent Millay

Known to her friends as Vincent, Edna St Vincent Millay had a notable and notorious career in the first half of the twentieth century.

She was born in 1892 in Rockland, Maine, one of three girls. Their mother, Cora, separated from her gambler husband when Edna was six and worked as a nurse to bring up her daughters herself. She encouraged all of them to take an interest in literature and music and urged them to be both independent and ambitious, qualities not commonly thought appropriate for women at that time.

Edna wrote from an early age and in 1912, encouraged by her mother, she entered a poem, *Renascence*, in a poetry competition and won fourth place. It is an intense piece of writing in which the poet, lying on her back looking up at the sky, imagines infinity. The poem was published in *The Lyric Year* and brought her instant recognition. It also helped her to win a scholarship to Vassar University, then an all-female institution.

She developed her writing at University and became very involved in the University Dramatic Society, performing, directing and writing plays for them. She graduated in 1917 and in the same year her first volume of poetry was published. She had also begun to write fiction under the pen-name of Nancy Boyd.

While she was at Vassar, Millay developed close relationships with several women, and these continued after she graduated and established herself among the artistic fraternity of New York's Greenwich Village. It was a Bohemian life-style. She was openly bi-sexual and had relationships with a number of other writers and artists. The writer Floyd Dell asked her to marry him, but she refused to be tied down. She joined the then celebrated Princetown Players and pursued her theatre interests. Her first verse play, *The Lamp and the Bell*, dealt openly with a lesbian relationship, as did one of the pieces in her next volume of verse, *A Few Figs from Thistles*, which inevitably drew a controversial response.

Between 1921 and 1923 Millay travelled round Europe, commissioned to write a series of pieces for *Vanity Fair*. The articles were published in book form with the title *Distressing*

Dialogues. Her next volume, *The Harp Weaver*, won the Pulitzer Prize. This was followed by the libretto for what became a popular American opera, *The King's Henchman*.

In 1923 she unexpectedly married a wealthy Dutch businessman, Eugen Boissevain, who was himself a firm believer in feminism. The marriage, according to Millay, was 'sexually open' but it clearly worked, as they remained together for twenty-six years until Boissevain's death in 1949. Boissevain gave up his own business to become his wife's manager. He organised public readings of her poetry and regular readings on radio, through which she became widely known. Public appearances became fewer after 1936, following Millay's involvement in a car accident.

In the 1920s Millay became more openly involved in political issues. She joined the campaign against the execution of Nicola Sacco and Bartholemo Vanzetti, who had been wrongly convicted of burglary and murder, and she was briefly arrested for taking part in a demonstration. Several of her poems of this period focus on the case. She was also a firm pacifist and one of her most notable poems in the 1934 book, *Wine from the Grapes*, is *Conscientious Objector* which expresses her feelings vividly using a horse as a dramatic image of death.

With the advent of the Second World War Millay abandoned her pacifism to support America's war effort. It was a difficult time, as much of her husband's money was lost when the Nazis invaded Holland, and Millay herself was beginning to suffer from the effects of years of alcohol and drug abuse. In 1944 she was hospitalised for several months with a nervous breakdown.

Millay died less than a year after her husband in 1950. Their home at Austerlitz, New York has since become a National Historic Landmark, and in 1973 Millay's sister, Norma, established there the 'Millay Colony for the Arts' to provide support for struggling young writers and artists.

Among other poets of the 1920s and 30s Millay stands out as a writer who created a bridge between past and present, rather than attempting to make a break with tradition, as did Modernists such as Ezra Pound. She wrote free verse with ease and vigour, but many would say her best work is in her use of the rigorous sonnet form. The collection *Fatal Interview,* which contains fifty-two sonnets tracing the progress of a love affair, is, according to the writer and critic Edmund Wilson, among the greatest poetry of the twentieth century. There may however be some bias in his judgement, as Wilson was Millay's one-time lover!

Nevertheless, there is no doubt that Millay did master the sonnet, both in its Italian and English forms, and she showed that it could express emotion and ideas in modern language. *If I should learn...* is a clear example of her skill. She tells how she would react if her lover did not return:

> I should but watch the station lights rush by
> With a more careful interest on my face;
> Or raise my eyes and read with greater care
> Where to store furs and how to treat the hair.

Millay is also flexible with the rhyme scheme when it helps to support the mood and thought. 'What lips my lips have kissed...' escapes from the expected rhymes in the sextet because it helps her to convey the sense of loneliness and disillusion as she realises that she can no longer remember

> what arms have lain
> Under my head till morning.

Millay was once asked what five things she thought necessary for a happy life and she responded:

'A job – something at which you must work for a few hours everyday. An assurance that you will have at least one meal a day for at least the next week. An opportunity to visit all the countries of the world, to acquaint yourself with the customs and their culture. Freedom in religion, or freedom from all religions, as you prefer. An assurance that no door is closed to you – that you may climb as high as you can build your ladder.'

Before ill-health began to dominate her life, Millay could be said to have had all these, and she was able to climb her ladder because she was part of a society that allowed her to have a greater freedom than that enjoyed by women of an earlier generation.

Pablo Neruda

Pablo Neruda was born Neftali Ricardo Reyes in Chile in 1904. He became perhaps the greatest poet to write in Spanish in the twentieth century.

His mother died shortly after he was born and he and his father, a railway worker, moved to the town of Temuco in Southern Chile. His father was involved in opening up the area for the new railways, which in effect meant cutting down an expanse of forest, something that for Neruda became one of many instances of man subduing nature for his own ends.

Neruda wrote poetry from the age of ten and at thirteen began to contribute articles to the daily paper, *La Manana*. The pseudonym Pablo Neruda first appeared in a literary journal in 1920, Neruda being the surname of the then famous Czech writer Jan Neruda. The name Pablo Neruda was legally adopted by the poet in 1946.

Neruda went to University in Santiago to study French and published his first volume of poetry while he was still an undergraduate. His second book, *Twenty Poems of Love and a Song of Despair*, appeared three years later in 1924 and earned him considerable praise. By the age of twenty Neruda had become a full-time writer, but money was short, and he made just enough to live on by taking a series of appointments as Honorary Consul in various Far Eastern countries. This was a period of loneliness and isolation for him, and it is reflected in his poetry of the time.

In 1933 Neruda took up a consular post in Spain, which marked a turning point for him. He published a new volume of poetry, *Residence on Earth*, largely a product of his experiences in the Far East, and this gained him recognition in Europe. The influence of Surrealism can also be seen, which he encountered as he met many of Spain's leading writers, including Federico Garcia Lorca. Through these new friends he also became involved in politics and Lorca's assassination in 1936 prompted a vigorous reaction from Neruda. As a result of his involvement he lost his consular position but this served only to harden his resolve to fight against repression.

He was eventually given a consular appointment in Mexico, but it was not long before he returned to Chile, became a member of the Communist Party and was elected Senator. The threats which followed his open criticism of the government's repressive regime forced him to go into hiding and he spent two years living in a variety of 'safe' houses. Throughout this time he continued to write and his major poem *Canto General* was published in Mexico in 1950 after he had fled Chile on horseback with the manuscript in his saddle bag. It has been described as the major Southern American epic, dealing as it does with the history and nature of the people and the place. The central section of the work, *The Heights of Macchu Picchu*, was inspired by a trip to the Inca ruins in 1943.

From this time Neruda enjoyed fame and translations of his work into many languages brought him some wealth. He continued with both his writing and his political activities and in 1955 he married Matilda Urrutia, a union which lasted until Neruda's death and which encouraged him to return to writing love poetry.

In 1970 the socialist Salvador Allende became President of Chile and Neruda was appointed Ambassador to Paris. The following year he received the Nobel Prize for Literature but he was already suffering from cancer and he returned to Chile where he died in 1973, just after the death of Allende in a military coup. Neruda's funeral provided an occasion for a demonstration against the new regime and in retaliation his house in Santiago was looted and many of his papers destroyed.

Neruda's writing life spanned more than fifty years, so it is not surprising that his style and subject matter varied considerably in that time. His first and last writings, though, were love poems, the early ones poignantly considering an unhappy love affair, the later ones addressed to his wife, full of deep affection, sensuous and intense. More challenging to the reader are the poems of the late 1920s and 1930s, found in *Residence on Earth* which show the influence of Surrealism. This was an artistic movement which sought to explore beyond literal reality, using the juxtaposition of apparently random images and having little regard for regular syntax or poetic forms. Poems such as *Weak with the Dawn* build a powerful picture of despair and death:

> the rain falls on me, and is like me,
> it is like me in its raving, alone in the dead world,
> repulsed as it falls, and with no persistent form.

In the aftermath of Lorca's assassination and his involvement in the Spanish political struggle against Fascism, Neruda's verse took on a much more rhetorical style. Much of it is aimed directly at an audience of listeners as well as readers. It is from this period that Neruda began reading his poetry aloud at political meetings and his writing asks for a public response rather than the more personal expression of his earlier poems. The immediacy of *I Am Explaining a Few Things* is a striking example of his passionate appeal to ordinary people:

Face to face with you I have seen the blood
of Spain tower like a tide
to drown you in one wave
of pride and knives!

Some of his greatest work is found in *Canto General*. The different sections encompass a variety of styles, from descriptive to satiric, and much of it is concerned with the relationship between man and nature and celebrates the ordinary working man, a baker, a carpenter, in his everyday tasks. Increasingly Neruda became a 'poet of the people' whose daily life he saw as being more in tune with nature. And, as always, he is aware of the immense power of words, which he affirms:

give glass-quality to glass, blood to blood,
and life to life itself.

Muriel Stuart

Muriel Stuart has an unusual claim to fame. She was hailed by fellow poet Hugh MacDiarmid as the best woman poet of the Scottish Renaissance. However, despite her surname, Muriel Stuart was English and never even visited Scotland! There is also no evidence of any connection between her and MacDiarmid but his affirmation led to some of her work being included in Scottish anthologies of the mid-twentieth century.

She was in fact born Muriel Stuart Irwin in 1885 in Norbury, South London and although her father had some Scottish forbears there were no family links with Scotland. After leaving school she went to study Art and Design at Croydon School of Art, and then went to work for publishers, first Heinemann and then Herbert Jenkins, where she remained through the war years. She began writing poetry and several of her poems reflect the horror and waste of the First World War.

She became a founder member of the PEN Organisation, which was set up in 1921 by Mrs Dawson Scott to promote international co-operation and understanding between writers. The first President was John Galsworthy and Muriel Stuart was present at the first dinner, where someone made the remark that she 'not only is a poet but looks it'!

Her first published poems appeared during the war years in the journal *The English Review*. Her first collection, *Christ at Carnival* was published by Herbert Jenkins in 1916. In all she produced five volumes of verse, all of which received critical praise at the time. Thomas Hardy is recorded as having described some of her poems as 'superlative'. It seems surprising therefore that she is almost forgotten today; her poems do not appear in anthologies and few people have even heard of her. Her last book of poems, merely entitled *Selected Poems*, was published in 1927. Why she ceased to write poetry is uncertain but her love of gardening led her to produce two books on gardens in the 1930s. She died in 1967 without publishing anything further.

It is hardly surprising that, given these circumstances, information about Muriel Stuart's life and work is difficult to find. However, the assumption that she was Scottish led to a small Scottish publisher, James Robertson of Kettillonia, producing a slim anthology of some of her best work, including the poetic dialogue, *In the Orchard*. This piece explores one of Muriel Stuart's favourite themes, the relationship between a man and a woman and the frustration and sadness of women who are treated as playthings. The directness of the dialogue gives the poem a remarkably modern feel.

Another recurrent subject was nature and, not unexpectedly for a garden lover, the imagery is frequently drawn from plants and flowers. Outstanding among these poems is *The Seed Shop* with its powerful final stanza:

Here in their safe and simple house of death,
Sealed in their shells a million roses leap;
Here I can blow a garden with my breath,
And in my hand a forest lies asleep.

Jonathan Swift

Swift is remembered today as the author of *Gulliver's Travels,*
a children's adventure story of a voyage to the imaginary lands
of the Lilliputians and the Brobdingnagians, but this is in fact a
very limited view of both the book and the man.

Swift was born in Dublin in 1667. His parents were English
but his father died before he was born and he and his mother
were dependent on a rich uncle. Swift was sent to Kilkenny
Grammar School and later Trinity College, Dublin, where he
was a contemporary of the future dramatist William Congreve.

After graduation, Swift became household secretary to the
influential writer and politician Sir William Temple, who then
lived near London. Swift remained in that position until
Temple's death in 1699.

During this time he became tutor to Esther Johnson, whose
mother was a companion to Temple's sister. Swift and Esther
developed a warm friendship which continued till her death in
1728. She is better remembered as Stella, the name Swift
gave her when later he wrote her a long series of letters.

Following Temple's death, Swift went back to Ireland as
secretary and chaplain (he had taken orders in 1694) to Lord
Bookley. He then took a small parish near Dublin, with Esther
and her mother settling near by.

Throughout this time Swift's reputation as a satirical writer
on contemporary and political issues was growing. *The Tale
of a Tub*, published in 1704, is an entertaining allegory on the
differences between the Roman Catholic, Lutheran and
Calvinist Churches and their deviation from Christian truth as

epitomised by the Church of England. Swift was a sincere and committed Anglican, and indeed transferred his political allegiance from Whig to Tory when the former party refused to take an interest in Church matters. The Tories for their part saw a distinct advantage in having Swift's sharp wit on their side. Swift spent three years in London from 1710, ran the Tory journal *The Examiner*, and wrote a number of influential pamphlets. This was a time before newspapers had become established, and political views were communicated through pamphlets and essays in popular journals. Swift became friends with other Tory writers such as Alexander Pope and John Gay and was a respected member of the 'Scriblerus Club', whose members produced the supposed memoirs of the foolish and pedantic Martin Scriblerus. Swift also kept up a correspondence with 'Stella', revealing his affection for her and also expressing his true opinions of the people he met with in London. These letters were published after Swift's death as *Journal to Stella*.

As a rather poor reward for his endeavours after the Tories were returned to power, Swift was made Dean of St Patrick's Cathedral, Dublin, where he spent the rest of his life.

Gulliver's Travels was first published anonymously in 1726. The book is in fact a political satire and characters and events were easily recognisable to his contemporaries. Edited, it is the first two books of this work which have become the children's classic. The third is a satire on science and is not so accessible, not having the plausible story-lines of the first two books. The whole text was very successful when published, and it was followed in 1729 by *A Modest Proposal*, a biting satire on the attitudes of the rich. His ironic suggestion was that the children of the poor be raised and slaughtered as food for the wealthy!

In later years Swift suffered increasingly from crippling headaches, and eventually died in 1745, having outlived many of his contemporaries. He left his money to found a hospital in Dublin for the insane – this institution still exists today as St Patrick's Psychiatric Hospital.

Swift, in common with all the most distinguished writers of his period, was a political animal. Parliament had, by the end of the seventeenth century, achieved much greater autonomy than before and for the first time two distinct political parties began to emerge – Tories (mainly the old aristocracy and gentry) and Whigs (merchant and middle classes). Politics gained a wider audience and writers of the period were drawn in to support and publicise different points of view. It can be difficult today to appreciate some of the literature of this time as we are not familiar with the issues and personalities involved. Neither do we respond easily to the prevalent style. In all the arts, classicism was dominant, which explains why the writers of the period are often referred to as the Augustans, named after the Roman Emperor Augustus, in whose reign the greatest Latin poetry was written. The aim was for 'correctness', for balance, symmetry and elegance without unnecessary ornamentation.

This is reflected in Swift's style, which is always precise and controlled, never impassioned. At his most satirical he takes an impersonal tone which often heightens the irony and therefore the impact of what he has to say. He is much better known as a writer of prose than poetry, but when he did write verse the same witty, impersonal style can be seen. He was fond of the tetrameter rhyming couplet form, in which his ideas flowed easily. The satire is usually less biting than in his prose but the subjects are still based on real people and events. Swift would have agreed with his friend Pope when he declared that

The proper study of mankind is man

and he proceeded to examine his fellows' foibles with wit and humour.

Isabel Allende

Isabel Allende's background is more colourful than that of most writers. She was born in Lima, Peru, in 1942. Her father was a Chilean diplomat, cousin to Salvador Allende, later to become President of Chile.

When Isabel was three, her mother separated from her father and returned with her three children to live with her parents in Santiago. Later her mother married another diplomat and the family moved to Bolivia and then Beirut. Isabel was educated in private schools as the family moved around, but in 1958, in response to the Suez Crisis, she was sent home to Chile. After leaving college, she took a job with the United Nations Food and Agricultural Organisation in Santiago and in 1962 she married an engineer, Miguel Frias, whom she had met at college. Her daughter, Paula, was born the following year.

She began to work as a journalist in 1964, writing for a Chilean woman's magazine as well as a children's journal. She also contributed to television shows and documentaries. A play, *El embajado*, was completed in 1972.

Meanwhile in 1970, Salvador Allende was elected the first socialist president of Chile. He remained in power until September 1973 when a military coup, led by General Pinochet, ousted Allende's government. Allende died, though it has never been confirmed whether he was assassinated or committed suicide to avoid capture. As a member of Allende's family and a vocal supporter of socialism, Isabel was threatened and was compelled to leave the country for Venezuela, where she found work as a school administrator. Some of the events and the mood of the Chilean people at this time provide a background to Eva Luna's story.

Isabel Allende's first novel began as a long letter to her grandfather who was dying. It turned into *The House of*

Spirits which was published in 1982. *Of Love and Shadows* and *Eva Luna* quickly followed.

In 1988, following her divorce from Miguel Frias, Isabel married an American, Willie Gordon, and went to live in California where she has resided ever since. However she has returned several times to Chile since democracy was restored in 1990.

Tragedy struck in 1992 when Isabel's daughter, Paula, suffered a painful death from porphyria. Isabel survived the trauma of watching her daughter die by writing about it in *Paula*, which Isabel regards as the most important book she has written. She was then able to start writing stories again and *Portrait in Sepia* and *Daughter of Fortune* followed. Her latest book is *My Invented Country*, published in 2003.

Isabel Allende's family have played a significant role in Chilean politics and it is not surprising that a number of them have proved quite colourful characters, some of whom have provided the starting point for characters in her books. The most notable of these are Esteban Trueba and Clara de Valle in *The House of Spirits* who are based on Isabel's grandparents. An uncle has been a significant influence on the creation of more than one paternalistic figure, a character type found in several of her books. Riad Halabi takes on this role when he takes Eva back to his home in *Eva Luna*. Family life, both past and present is also a recurring theme. So also are characters who are on the periphery of social interaction – the outsiders. This is particularly significant in *Daughter of Fortune* which is about the American gold rush, but taken from the point of view of the Mexicans who owned the land and who were ousted by the more powerful and determined Americans.

Moments of humour and vivid description blend with drama and episodes of harsh reality to make Isabel Allende's books exciting reading.

Peter Carey

Peter Carey, who has the distinction of having twice won the Booker Prize, was born in 1943 in Bacchus March, a small town in the Australian state of Victoria. His parents sent him to the prestigious Geelong Grammar School. This was followed by time at Monash University in Melbourne studying Science but he soon realised that he was not cut out to be a scientist and left without a degree.

After university Carey found work writing advertising copy, a task at which he proved very successful. This was followed by a period in London before a return to Australia, this time to Sydney. His skill as a copy writer earned him a living and also provided the background to his first novel, *Bliss,* published in 1981, in which his main character wakes up from an operation and thinks that all his past life was lived in Hell.

In the 1980s Carey moved to New York with his wife and two sons, where he still lives and teaches creative writing at New York University. He does, however, remain very much an Australian. The history of Australia and what it means to be Australian inform all his major novels. *Illywacker*, which appeared in 1985, takes its name from a colloquial Australian word for a con man, and it tells much of the history of Australia in the twentieth century through the often comic experiences of Herbert Badgery, a self-confessed liar, whose adventures are partly based on the travels that Carey's grandfather undertook as one of the first Australian postmen. Perhaps strangely, this book won an award for the best Australian Science Fiction novel of 1986. Carey cannot truly be classed as a Science Fiction writer, but he does draw on elements characteristic of that genre as fact and fantasy so often mingle in Badgery's unlikely stories.

This meeting of fantasy and reality is also found in Carey's next book *Oscar and Lucinda,* which won him his first

Booker prize. The love story of the two main characters is set within an account of the introduction of Christianity to the outback. That Carey views this occurrence with a slightly jaundiced eye might be inferred from the 'missionary' Oscar initially proving the existence of God through gambling! Lucinda has inherited a glass factory and she and Oscar create a glass cathedral which Oscar then spectacularly fails to transfer to his mission station. The demise of the cathedral is echoed in the failure of Oscar and Lucinda's union. The book has been made into a successful film with Ralph Fiennes as Oscar.

Jack Maggs takes a step further back in history to the world of the first convicts to arrive in Australia. Jack Maggs is in fact Dickens' convict Magwitch from *Great Expectations*, who makes money and secretly returns to England. This book won the Commonwealth Writers' Award, and there was some controversial publicity when Carey declined to meet the Queen to receive his prize.

True History of the Kelly Gang was published in 2000, a study of the notorious bush ranger and bank robber, Ned Kelly, who was hanged in 1880 for shooting a police officer. The starting point for the book was Kelly's only surviving letter and from this Carey creates an amazingly believable first person narrative in the form of letters and journals that Ned Kelly writes for the daughter he never in the end saw. Carey said that he drew on the memories of his childhood in a small provincial town, particularly his recollection of the way people actually spoke, to create Kelly's distinctive voice. The reader has to tune in to the style which, true to Kelly's knowledge and experiences, is direct but uses minimal punctuation and is at times ungrammatical. The result is surprisingly authentic and moods of excitement, comedy and pathos follow each other all coloured by Ned's personality. In spite of the lack of punctuation this book is perhaps more easily accessible than some of Carey's earlier work, in which the style is often complex as he tackles large issues with serious intent.

True History of the Kelly Gang won Carey the Booker and the Commonwealth Writers' Prize for the second time, an acknowledgement that he is one of the most powerful novelists writing in English today.

My Life as a Fake, published in 2003, is based on a notorious literary hoax, but Carey's novel goes beyond the original events to explore, often through fantasy, what makes a true and original work of literature.

George Eliot

George Eliot, novelist, appeared in 1857. She had in fact been born as Mary Ann Evans thirty-eight years before this in Warwickshire, the last of three children. From the age of six she attended boarding school with her elder sister, first in Nuneaton and then in Coventry, where she encountered evangelical beliefs. She proved to be intelligent and keen to learn, but had to leave school at sixteen when her mother died. Her elder sister married the next year and Mary Ann was left as her father's housekeeper. She did, however, continue to educate herself.

In 1841 Mary Ann and her father moved to Coventry where she quickly gained entry to a circle of progressive intellectuals. Encouraged by the questioning of her friends, she found her own religious doubts, which had begun at school, hardening into agnosticism. It was not until after her father's death in 1849 that she was really free to pursue her own interests and beliefs.

She met John Chapman, the radical publisher of the *Westminster Review,* and she began to write. In 1851 she went to London as assistant editor on the journal. Here she met the writer and intellectual George Henry Lewes and they quickly developed a close relationship. Lewes was separated from his wife, and, in 1854 he and Mary Ann decided to live together, a momentous decision in strictly moralistic Victorian society. When she admitted the relationship to her brother, all contact with her family was cut off. In spite of the perceived immorality, Lewes and Mary Ann where accepted by the intellectuals of the day, and the relationship lasted until Lewes' death in 1878.

It was Lewes who encouraged his companion to turn to fiction, and with the appearance of *Scenes from Clerical Life* in Blackwood's magazine in 1857, the pseudonym George Eliot was born. This was a protection against the puritanical strictures of the Victorians, who saw a woman's place as quite definitely in the home; a woman writer might not be taken seriously. In this she was in good company – the Bronte sisters had already published under the names of Ellis, Currer and Acton Bell.

The short stories were quickly followed by the novels *Adam Bede, The Mill on the Floss* and *Silas Marner,* but it is generally acknowledged that her greatest achievement is the all-embracing *Middlemarch* which appeared in 1871–2.

Two years after Lewes' death Eliot agreed to marry an old friend, Johnny Cross. They moved into a house in Cheyne Walk, Chelsea, in December, but two weeks later Eliot developed a fever and died on 22nd December, aged sixty-one. She was buried in Highgate Cemetery next to Lewes. Cross later became her first biographer.

It is possible to claim that George Eliot is the first modern novelist. Some would say that she is *the* greatest English novelist. Parallels have been drawn between her work and that of Tolstoy and Turgenev. Certainly she influenced many writers who followed her, notably Henry James and D.H. Lawrence. Her stature comes from her highly intelligent approach combined with powers of both observation and imagination. Compared with other established novelists of the time like Dickens and Thackeray who viewed their work primarily as a source of entertainment, Eliot's writing had a greater seriousness of purpose. Indeed there are times when the 'issues' are perhaps over-emphasised. Eliot is keen that the reader should not make hasty judgements but for some readers the regular appearance of the author's comments can seem like an intrusion. However all her characters feel real and are set in a carefully constructed social situation, within which they have to work out their problems. The parallel problems of Dorothea and Lydgate in *Middlemarch* are largely determined by the society in which they live.

Of all Eliot's novels, *Middlemarch* creates the most comprehensive society for her characters. It is perhaps significant that her early books focus mainly on the dilemmas of one character, but the subtitle of *Middlemarch – A Study in Provincial Life* suggests a different approach. Here the multi-layered society of a small town becomes a protagonist and the characters are not able to escape from it. This is partly what makes the idealistic Ladislaw the least effective of Eliot's cast as he is a romanticised figure not quite of the real world.

Eliot drew on her own intimate knowledge of small town and rural society in creating her scenes, but never more thoroughly than in *Middlemarch*. The town is not unlike the Coventry in which she grew up and although the book was published in 1872, the action is set forty years before. She was keenly aware of the differences between the social classes and of the huge changes taking place in rural communities as agriculture gradually gave way to industry. The period of the novel coincides with the considerable unrest which led to the Reform Bill of 1832 (which offered the right to vote to a much greater number of the population) and personal experiences are always set against these wider political issues. In Eliot's most overtly political novel, *Felix Holt*, she wrote that, 'there is no private life which has not been determined by a wider public life'. Perhaps Eliot's greatest success is showing how this operates in all levels of society while maintaining the reader's interest and sympathy for individuals.

Henry James

Henry James was one of the great novelists whose life spanned the end of the nineteenth century and the early years of the twentieth. But was he English or American? He was born in America but lived most of his adult life in England, becoming a British citizen. This duality is at the heart of much of his writing.

Henry James was born in New York in 1843, the younger of two brothers. The elder, William, became a distinguished philosopher. Their father, the son of an Ulster immigrant, became a wealthy man and had striking, individualist views. Convinced that the usual educational channels produced dull and unthinking people, he travelled around Europe with his family and Henry attended schools in New York, London, Paris, Geneva, Boulogne and Bonn before entering Harvard University to read Law. This nomadic existence turned him into a spectator of life and for many years he found himself on the sidelines of whichever society he was living in. He began writing when he was a boy, using exercise books in which he would leave the fourth page blank to illustrate what he had written.

After university James had little inclination to settle for a career in law – he wanted to write. In late nineteenth-century America, this was still possible for someone with money. There was little competition and he made a living writing short stories and articles for any journal that would accept them. His unconventional upbringing made him long for a settled life, with order and tradition, so he headed for Europe, settling at first in Paris, where he met other writers, such as Flaubert and Turgenev. However, in 1876 he moved to England, living at first in London and eventually buying a house in Rye, Sussex, where he lived until his death in 1916.

James became a well-known figure in London society and must have led a hectic life; he recorded that in the winter of

1878 he accepted 107 invitations to social events! The move to Sussex gave him more time to concentrate on his writing. His first novel, *Roderick Hudson*, was published in 1875 and was well received. *Washington Square*, which has proved one of his most popular stories, appeared in 1880. It was subsequently turned into a Hollywood film and a stage play with the title *The Heiress*. He was a prolific writer, producing twenty novels, many of them published with his own prefaces. *Portrait of a Lady*, often regarded as his greatest work, appeared in 1881 but was followed by equally penetrating and carefully constructed novels, such as *What Maisie Knew*, *The Wings of a Dove* and *The Ambassadors*. His last book, *The Golden Bowl*, was published in 1904. By this time he had become a fully established English gentleman. In 1915 he was awarded the Order of Merit and in the same year became a British citizen.

We know an unusual amount about the creation of Henry James' novels as he prepared them meticulously and kept copious notes in exercise books. He also wrote prefaces to each work, and made revisions to his earliest writings when preparing them for a collected edition. His characters are presented in great detail and set in carefully constructed social backgrounds. He said that he viewed each novel as a self-contained entity which was also intended to achieve maximum universal significance.

That the reader can accept James' characters as both individuals and as symbols comes from his extremely complex writing style. The length of James' sentences is notorious, as he packs layers of meaning into visual and metaphorical detail. Sometimes the meaning can be hard to unravel and there are critics who find the writing in the later works too verbose. The results however are characters who have much greater stature and depth than one would expect from the social context of the stories. So Isabel Archer in *Portrait of a Lady* is not only a young American in search of culture and more than just a socially successful marriage; she becomes a symbol for youthful promise and potential. Milly Thrale in *The Wings of a Dove* is given tragic stature by having, in addition to youth and wealth, a fatal illness (never actually specified) which dooms her to an early death.

The central characters of all James' best known novels are women – American women – free from the social restraints often experienced by English heroines. They are also innocent and naïve: by coming to Europe they become victims of the apparently sophisticated and cultured society to which they aspire to belong. Catherine in *Washington Square* is trapped by the much travelled, suave and socially adept Morris Townsend.

The cultural and social differences between American and European society are central to a Jamesian novel. James clearly felt more at home in Europe than America but he was American by birth and so had a slightly detached view of European society, acknowledging the desirable features but also the evils. James brought many of his American heroines to Europe because, as he saw it, America needed to learn what Europe had to offer in terms of history and tradition; however, there seems no reciprocal need for European characters to 'discover' America. Although there is a strong sense of right and wrong running through James' work, the distinction between the two is never clear cut. The Americans retain much of their self-belief and persist with what appears the right course of action even though it cannot possibly lead to happiness. Consequently Isabel Archer remains with the cold unloving Gilbert Osmond because she has married him, in spite of strong persuasion on the part of her former suitor Caspar Goodwood. Neither will Catherine Sloper be tempted to seek happiness a second time, once she has faced Morris Townsend's betrayal.

Bernard MacLaverty

Bernard MacLaverty was born in Belfast in 1942 and he continued to live there through some of the worst of the Troubles, until moving to Scotland in 1975.

After leaving school MacLaverty became a laboratory technician and it was ten years later that he decided to become a mature student at Queen's University, Belfast. He graduated with a degree in English in 1974 and became a teacher.

Scotland was pleasantly free from the tensions of Northern Ireland, and he and his family lived first in Edinburgh, then on the Isle of Islay, before settling in Glasgow.

His first publication was a book of short stories, *Secrets*, followed in 1980 by the novel *Cal*. Praise from critics encouraged him to give up his teaching job to devote more time to writing. The novel *Lamb* appeared in 1983 and in 1997 he wrote *Grace Notes*, which was short-listed for the Booker Prize. He has written three other volumes of short stories and several television plays. *Cal* and *Lamb* were both made into successful films, the former starring Liam Neeson. His latest novel, *The Anatomy School*, was published in 2001.

It is interesting to observe that although MacLaverty's published work has been written since his move to Scotland all his books draw on his Northern Irish background for themes and characters. *Cal* and *The Anatomy School* are both set in Belfast and *Grace Notes* moves between there and Scotland. Living in Northern Ireland in the 1950s and 60s definitely left its mark on MacLaverty. Resentment between Catholics and Protestants in the province built up over several generations, spilling over into violence, notably in the Falls Road area in Belfast. The British army were brought in to help keep the peace and were at first welcomed by Catholics. Fuelled by the fanaticism of the provisional Sinn Fein, terrorist wing of the

Irish Republican Army, whose aim was union with Southern Ireland at any price, Catholics turned against the British soldiers. Both sides took up arms and the Troubles began, escalating into the appalling events of 'Bloody Sunday' in 1972. Yet against this background people tried to lead normal lives.

MacLaverty experienced all this at first hand but what is noticeable about his attitude to Belfast is that he can write about the situation without sentimentality or moralising. Even in *Cal*, in which the IRA/Protestant conflict figures most prominently (the main character falls in love with a widow whose husband he killed), his concern is for individuals and judgements are not passed.

As well as setting part of the story in Belfast, *Grace Notes* also draws on MacLaverty's love of music. In addition to writing MacLaverty has also broadcast on Radio Three, the BBC's classical music station, and has been responsible for a classical music programme on BBC Scotland. He has acknowledged that in some ways music is more important to him than writing and this is certainly reflected in his sensitive portrayal of Catherine McKenna, the central character of *Grace Notes*. Catherine is a gifted composer, who has to struggle to achieve success against the ghosts of her Belfast upbringing, pregnancy and post-natal depression. Like all MacLaverty's writing, it is a story with much sadness in it, but there are also touches of humour and hope for the future when Catherine's symphony is finally performed.

Rohinton Mistry

With three novels and a book of short stories Mistry has joined a distinguished group of writers, including Vikram Seth, Arundhati Roy and Salman Rushdie, who have written evocatively about life in India.

Mistry was born in Bombay in 1952 and grew up there in a three-roomed flat with his parents and three siblings. As a boy he showed an aptitude for creative writing, but was also interested in sport and music. He taught himself to play the harmonica and then the guitar. By the time he left school he was performing Bob Dylan songs in public concerts.

Mistry came from a Parsi family, members of a small sect who follow the teachings of Zoroastra and whose ancestors came to India from Iran in the eighteenth century to avoid persecution. There is still a sizeable and close-knit Parsi community in Bombay and Mistry draws on his experiences of this life in his books.

Shortly after graduating from Bombay University in Maths and Economics in 1975, Mistry decided to emigrate to Canada. He left just after Indira Ghandi declared a State of Emergency throughout the country. Many people were persecuted and imprisoned as Indira Ghandi fought to hold on to power, even though a High Court Judge had ruled her election as Prime Minister to be invalid. This anarchic period provides a background to the events in *A Fine Balance*, Mistry's second novel.

Mistry initially worked in a bank in Toronto and rose to supervisor status in the Customer Services department. However, he did not find the work satisfying and began a four-year part-time course in English and Philosophy at Toronto University. In 1983 he began to write short stories in his spare time, and taking two days sick leave from the bank, wrote *One Sunday* with which he won the University Hart House Literary Competition. He won again the following year, and his story appeared in *The New Press Anthology: Best Canadian Short Fiction*.

In 1984, on receiving a grant from the Canadian government, Mistry resigned from the bank to write full time. In 1987 Penguin published his collection of short stories *Swimming Lessons and Other Stories from Firozsha Baag*. These are eleven interconnected tales of life in a Parsi apartment block and they focus on the issues of religion, poverty and exclusion.

His first novel *Such a Long Journey* appeared in 1991, was short-listed for the Booker Prize and won the Commonwealth Writers' Award. It is set in India in the early 1970s, during the war over territory that is now Bangladesh. The book was made into a film in 1998. Mistry won the Commonwealth Writers' Award again in 1995 with *A Fine Balance*. When this too was nominated for the Booker Prize, Germaine Greer provoked a furore with some ill-judged comments on the book, which she had disliked. She is quoted as describing it as 'a Canadian book about India. What could be worse?' Mistry, having lived all his formative years in India, and who revisits regularly, responded with one word – 'asinine'.

Mistry's latest novel, *Family Matters*, came out in 2002 and looks at the universal problem faced by a family when the elderly father suffers from Parkinson's disease and becomes bed-ridden.

Critics have compared Mistry to Salman Rushdie, but although *Midnight's Children* and *A Fine Balance* appeared in the same year, and both use Gandhi's State of Emergency as a background, Rushdie writes about the reactions of the Muslim middle class Indians, while Mistry looks at the lives of the poor. In his social realism and linear narrative, Mistry has also been compared to Charles Dickens, though Mistry himself denies the influence, confessing to only a limited acquaintance with the nineteenth-century writer.

In *A Fine Balance* Mistry evokes the sordid, over-crowded, poverty-stricken but vibrant life of Bombay, though he never actually names the city. The four protagonists come from widely different backgrounds, but through a period of changing fortunes they form what at first seems an unlikely alliance. In the course of becoming a kind of 'family' unit Mistry shows that individuals can forget about caste, religion and politics in difficult times. There is humour as well as desperate hardship and tragedy in the story, but in the vitality and doggedness of Ishvar and Omprakesh, the two tailors, there is always hope for the future.

Dorothy Parker

There can be few writers who are so distinctly a product of their generation as Dorothy Parker. She was born Dorothy Rothschild in New Jersey in 1893 (her family were unrelated to the banking Rothschilds) but her mother died when she was young and she was brought up in New York by a strict father and step-mother. She was educated at a Catholic convent school, but never felt she fitted in there.

Her writing career began when she sent some poems to the editor of *Vogue* magazine, on the strength of which she was offered a job writing captions for magazine illustrations. After about a year she moved on to *Vanity Fair*, becoming its theatre critic even though she had not previously shown any particular interest in this field.

In 1917 she married Edwin Parker. The marriage did not last, but Dorothy continued to use the name Parker, which she preferred to her own with its Jewish associations.

Meanwhile, her barbed reviews, full of neatly turned phrases, soon gained her a reputation in New York society. She belonged to the exclusive Algonquin Round Table, an informal luncheon club and a social and literary coterie, becoming known as its wittiest and often its only female member.

When the *New Yorker* magazine was started in 1925 Parker helped to shape its character. As well as some acerbic theatre and book reviews she began to contribute short stories which fast became popular. She continued to write, intermittently, for the publication for twenty years.

In her forays into society she met some of America's leading writers, such as Ernest Hemingway and F. Scott Fitzgerald but she was never part of their intellectual elite. She was, however, an extremely popular writer. When she published her first volume of poems, *Enough Rope*, it quickly became a best-seller.

In 1930 Parker met and married Alan Campbell, an actor and writer. The couple went to Hollywood as a writing team and produced screen plays for a number of popular films. Together with Lillian Hellman and Dashiel Hammett, Parker helped to found the Screenwriters' Guild. It was at this period, however, that she became involved in left-wing politics. Her bold speeches against Fascism resulted in a decrease in commissions for her and her husband. Their promising careers faltered, as did their marriage. They divorced in 1947, remarried three years later, separated again and eventually came together for the years before Campbell's death in 1963. Dorothy continued to use the surname Parker throughout the relationship.

Dorothy returned to New York after the failure of the Hollywood project and continued to write, but her approach did not fit in with the changed attitudes of Post-War society. Her last significant writing was in fact a play, *Ladies of the Corridor*, which dealt with widows compelled to live out their lives in a residential hotel. It was not a success when performed, even though the Parker wit still produced some snappy lines. Her comment on the play was, 'It was the only thing I ever did that I was proud of.' The subject matter turned out to be prophetic however, as Dorothy herself lived her last years in just such a hotel as she created. She died, lonely and forgotten, in 1967, leaving her estate to Martin Luther King.

Dorothy Parker's heyday was the 1920s. It was an age of frivolity in many ways and for women in particular a period of permissiveness compared with that of previous generations. Bobbed hair, short skirts, bold make-up and smoking set the tone for the New York social set, as they did in London. Into this scene Parker's wit and perceptiveness fitted perfectly and she became a leading light among her literary set. However, despite success and wealth she was rarely happy; she often drank heavily, had numerous affairs and attempted suicide three times. Much of her work has an underlying preoccupation with death. Parker clearly admired anyone who died young, especially if they took their own lives. 'People ought to be young or dead,' she said.

Parker's writing is evocative of the time. Her verse captures the spirit of the age but it is her short stories that show a keener understanding of human nature. Her wit still appears sharp and fresh and she has a special flare for striking opening lines which grab the reader's attention. Her mockery is aimed at those who are self-important and vain; the underdog is never ridiculed.

As she grew older the world moved on and fashions changed but Parker could not move with them. When success faded, her wit became more bitter and was often directed at friends who where alienated by her caustic comments.

Bram Stoker

Although Bram Stoker was quite a prolific writer, he is remembered today for one book only – *Dracula* – which has never been out of print since it was published in 1897.

Abraham Stoker was born in Dublin in 1847, the son of a civil servant and a mother who wrote and was known for her charity work. As a young child Bram, as he became known, suffered continual illness, unable to walk properly until he was seven. During this time, to keep her son entertained, his mother would often tell him horror stories. The reason for his ill-health is not known, but he made a remarkable recovery, went to the same school as Oscar Wilde and continued on to

Trinity College, Dublin, where he gained the reputation as a leading athlete.

He read Maths at Trinity before following his father into the civil service, though it was not an occupation that he enjoyed, being more interested in writing and the theatre. He began writing theatre reviews for Dublin papers, often unpaid, to try and make a name for himself. He also wrote short stories at this time, though his first book, published in 1878, had the uninspiring title of *The Duties of Clerks of Petty Sessions in Ireland*.

A turning point in Stoker's career was a visit to Dublin by the famous actor Henry Irving in 1876. Stoker saw him in *Hamlet*, was overwhelmed, wrote a rave review and was able to meet the great man. This was the beginning of a long and close relationship, for when, two years later, Irving decided to take over the Lyceum Theatre in London, he invited Stoker to be his manager. Stoker remained in the job for twenty-seven years; quite a feat as Irving was a demanding and often irascible employer.

In 1878 Stoker married the young actress Florence Balcombe, whom he is believed to have met through Oscar Wilde. The marriage was not a success, and although the two continued to live together after the birth of their only son in 1889, neither remained faithful to the other.

In spite of the long hours he worked in the theatre Stoker continued to write, producing eighteen books in all. These were moderately successful at the time, but it was *Dracula* which made him famous.

Stoker continued to work at the Lyceum until his death in 1912, the result of years of over-work, though it has been suspected the immediate cause was syphilis.

Dracula belongs to the genre of the Gothic novel. The term 'Gothic' originally referred to a style of medieval architecture with high pointed arches. Gothic novels would therefore be set in old (often ruined) castles or monasteries, and writers would use the darkness and gloom of the buildings to help them create an atmosphere of terror and high drama. The first notable book of this genre was Horace Walpole's *The Castle of Otranto* which appeared in 1764 and began a vogue for such tales. The book was sufficiently popular for Jane Austen to be able to apply some gentle mockery to its over-blown style in *Northanger Abbey*.

The term 'Gothic' has come to have an extended meaning, encompassing any horrific, supernatural stories with a claustrophobic atmosphere. The best known is Mary Shelley's *Frankenstein*, and the influences of the genre can be seen in the writings of Sir Walter Scott and Robert Louis Stevenson both of whom would have been familiar to Stoker. He would certainly have known the story of *Carmilla* by fellow Irish writer Sheridan Le Fanu, whose central character is a female vampire. It is easy to see why the excitement and suspense of such tales would capture the imagination of the reading public, as detective and mystery stories do today. At the time Stoker was writing the reading public increased. The Education Act of 1870 provided compulsory primary education for all, which vastly increased the number of people able to read and to whom an exciting adventure story would appeal.

Stoker certainly took great care with *Dracula*. The settings and background were all thoroughly researched. He went to the British Museum to find out more about Transylvania and he visited Whitby, where part of the book is set and even used the exact inscriptions on some of the tombstones in the churchyard. The story is mainly placed in London, and this was naturally well-known to Stoker. All this helps to give the book a grounding in reality, unlike the traditional Gothic setting. The main characters, Dracula apart, are ordinary people, a professional solicitor and two doctors.

Dracula himself was based on a real Balkan Prince, Vlad Tepes, and the lore of vampirism had been explored in detail.

The novel gains in immediacy by the style of writing. It is not a straight-forward narrative, but unfolds through letters and diaries and the several strands only gradually come together, helping to sustain the suspense. The characters are revealed through their writing, with Dracula remote, only seen through others.

Some typically Victorian attitudes are upheld in the novel, notably the firmly distinguished roles society saw for men and women. Women are the weaker sex, to be protected, but are also a force for good. It is interesting that it is the two women who are in part taken over by Dracula, thus blurring the divide between good and evil. It is through them that the sexual nature of vampirism is revealed. Vampirism can be 'caught' and it is the women who are contaminated, in scenes remarkably erotic for a respectable Victorian novel. They were acceptable because, of course, vampires were not regarded as human, and Dracula himself came from Eastern Europe, an uncivilised and inferior place to the empire-conscious Victorians. Furthermore, the evil is finally defeated largely by the logical, scientific methods of Van Helsing, indicating the degree of respect given to science and reason at this time. Van Helsing's painstaking deductions are in places reminiscent of those of Sherlock Holmes.

Dracula holds its place today as a prime tale of horror and suspense. It still captures the imagination and Bram Stoker's name is commemorated in the annual Bram Stoker Awards given by the Horror Writers' Association. There is a statue of him in Trinity College, Dublin and Ireland even has an official 'Dracula Association'.

William Shakespeare

Much of Shakespeare's life is shrouded in mystery so it is important that you conduct your own research in order to draw your own conclusions.

There are numerous books published on Shakespeare's life, times and works. The following publications will provide you with more than enough information for your discussion with the examiner.

Claybourne, A & Treays, R – The World of Shakespeare (Usborne Publishing)

Dobson, M & Wells, S – The Oxford Companion to Shakespeare (Oxford University Press)

Harrison, G B – Introducing Shakespeare (Penguin)

Granville-Barker, H – Prefaces to Shakespeare (Nick Hern Books)

Laroque, F – Shakespeare: Court, Crowd and Playhouse (New Horizons Series, Thames and Hudson)

Michell, J – Who Wrote Shakespeare? (Thames and Hudson)

Tillyard, E M W – The Elizabethan World Picture (Pimlico)

Wood, M – In Search of Shakespeare (BBC Publications)